The Long Island Company

A History of Company H, 1st Regiment of US Sharpshooters

CHRIS SCHNUPP

Front cover photo courtesy of Brian T. White

Copyright © 2015 Chris Schnupp

All rights reserved.

ISBN: 1512330639

ISBN-13: 978-1512330632

DEDICATION

This book is dedicated to those that served, and sacrificed in order to form a "more perfect union."

CONTENTS

	Acknowledgments	i
1	Introduction	Pg #11
2	April 1861	Pg #13
3	August 1861	Pg #18
4	1862	Pg #36
5	1863	Pg # 63
6	1864	Pg # 74
7	1865	Pg # 82
8	After the War	Pg # 84
9	Biographical Sketches	Pg # 99
10	Author's Note	Pg # 166
11	Bibliography	Pg # 167

Images

Photo	Courtesy of:	Page
George Hastings	Brian T. White	Front Cover
John Schermerhorn Uniform	Richard Smallwood-Roberts	Pg #27
George Hastings	Brian T. White	Pg #87
William Winthrop	1890 Class Album USMA Library	Pg #88
Frederick T. Peet	Diary of Frederick T Peet 1899	Pg #89
Michael McGeough	Richard Smallwood-Roberts	Pg #90
John Schermerhorn		Pg #91
Orrin Doty	Ken Harris	Pg #92
Barnard Gardner	David Moore	Pg #93
George F Hall		Pg #94
Edward J. Carmick	West Point Museum Coll., USMA	Pg #95
Richard L. Boyd	Brian T. White	Pg. #96
Sylvester Lawson	Sean T. Otis	Pg. #97
Harry D. Tyler	Brian T. White	Pg. #98

ACKNOWLEDGMENTS

There are many people to thank when conducting research on this level. First off, I would like to thank my family, Geraldine Aloise, Jeanne Schnupp, Jenn Schnupp and David Schnupp for constant support and encouragement. Additionally several Berdan historians: Richard Smallwood-Roberts, John Carey, Ben Bosley, David Rider, Brian T White, Richard Simmons, and Bill Skillman. Thanks also to Marlana Cook and Suzanne Christoff at the West Point Museum at the US Military Academy as well as living relatives of Company H: Ken Harris, Jack Cooley Clifford and David Moore. Special thanks to my close friends for continued support.

1 INTRODUCTION

"If my duty again calls me into a fight I shall go in cheerfully, coolly and without a thought of fear or danger" – Captain Hastings

The First U.S. Sharpshooters possessed unique qualities that went beyond their uniforms, accoutrements, and tactics. The soldiers of Company H were descended from a cross-section of America at the time. This was unique during the Civil War, since it was customary for a company to be recruited solely from a township and its neighboring rural outposts. Although their ancestors predominantly held traditional roles such as farmer or carpenter, the members of Company H held a variety of jobs and several had climbed the social ladder. Within the historic families of Company H were the founders of: Block Island, New York; Boston, Mass; Hartford, Connecticut; Milford, Connecticut; Wenham, Mass; and Winthrop, Mass. Other ancestors were responsible for establishing a railroad and a popular church of the time. Many still have names of towns and streets associated with them on Long Island such as

Lattingtown, Swezeytown, Tappan Ave, and Tooker Avenue. Although some ancestors were slave owners and others participated in the Salem Witch Trials, they were all helping to build America into a growing nation whose youth would come together to form Company H.

2 APRIL 1861

The nation's growth would unfortunately divide the country and pose a great challenge for its founders. The divide would eventually drive the country into a civil war.

In April of 1861, the president called for the state militias to send troops to defend the nation's capital. Lincoln anticipated Congress would approve additional calls for a larger volunteer army when they returned to session on July 4th. Based on this strategy, the president expanded his request to include additional regular army regiments (Army, 1999). Seeing the opportunity to raise regiments as a means of status, politicians, the social elite, and adventurous glory-seekers competed to gain commissions. Among them was Hiram Berdan, an inventor who proposed the idea that men armed with advanced weapons may use camouflage and employ guerilla style tactics that lead the colonists to victories in previous wars. The type of regiment Berdan had in mind would be a cross between dragoon and cavalry. These expert marksmen would be able to strike the enemy from a distance and move swiftly to the next target. What is interesting about this strategy is it was originally used in the army of 1812 by combining the riflemen of Daniel Morgan, the militia men of Frances Marion, and the rangers of Robert Rogers. In 1812, the federal government raised three regiments of riflemen who wore green and implemented advanced weapons and guerilla tactics to strike out at British forces. Their reputation as marksmen would strike fear into the hearts of the enemy before stepping onto a battlefield. In a time when tactics were still based on massing fire at a target by standing shoulder to shoulder and firing volleys, these riflemen would work in a loose formation, acting as skirmishers and parsed out in platoons where they were most needed.

Berdan's Sharpshooters would function in much the same way. Dark green uniforms would be used during the summer months to blend in with the foliage. During the winter months sharpshooters would add grey coats and hats to hide them among the fall leaves and snow. A new rifle would be used that was easier to reload and more accurate than the average musket. This would enable soldiers to increase fire on the enemy. Hiram Berdan, a wealthy New York inventor[1], also happened to be a renowned marksman himself. His

---
[1] Berdan invented a process for separating gold from ore, a mechanized bakery, a reaper, his own rifle and ammunition, submarine gun boats among others-he was

early demonstrations of the "sharpshooter test" would generally result in ten bullets grouped within a hand drawn caricature of Confederate President Jefferson Davis. With call of volunteers, Berdan figured he would be able to raise the defunct riflemen regiments as his own brigade. Berdan wanted to differentiate his command from the rest of the army. Seeking to fill as many regiments as possible, Berdan wanted to amass enough troops to create an independent command.

A foreshadowing of how his Civil War military career would run, Berdan's grand idea for a unit operating outside standard military control was not feasible. This unfortunate circumstance would be followed by Abraham Lincoln denying his request for promotion to Brigadier General (Berdan H. Letter to Abraham Lincoln November 27, 1862, 1862). Without possessing the independent command that he wanted, Berdan would have to work with the commanding officers to ensure that the sharpshooters were used effectively. Although it would still be a full year before the sharpshooter regiments would take the field, Berdan felt confident that it would be enough time to prove that his command would be valid and vital to the Union cause, eventually earning him a promotion and independent command.

Berdan and his officers would have to find and train the best marksmen in the north. A test was established to determine the

---

sued in April of 1860 for non-disclosure of patents that were being used in the bakery.

skills of the volunteers. It required that all applicants would have to hit a target from 200 yards five times at no more than 3 inches from the bull's-eye. With help from his secretary Berdan began circulating notices of recruitment and soon had enough officers to begin filling the first regiment of sharpshooters.

When the April call went up, the militias were the main source of immediate manpower that could be used to suppress a rebellion without congressional approval[2]. Very few organizations, however, were at the level of the vaunted 7th New York Militia. This was attributed to their excellent training and the elite social status of many of members of the "Silk Stocking Regiment." This regiment was established in 1806, and served as artillery in the war of 1812. It became the pre-eminent militia unit in the United States, and one of the first regiments to be mustered into service following the attack on Fort Sumter. They bargained for a 30 day enlistment instead of the standard 90 days that Lincoln requested. With space limited, privileged families vied for spots for their sons. Due to the statuses of their families, brothers William and Theodore Winthrop were mustered in with their good friend Robert Gould Shaw and brother-in-law Roswell Weston. The Winthrop brothers originally from

---

[2] There is widespread debate over legality of using the militia to suppress other states. The legal definition of an insurrection is: A rising or rebellion of citizens against their government usually manifested by acts of violence. Under federal law, it is a crime to incite, assist, or engage in such conduct against the United States. Within this definition is a grey area of whether a state could incite an insurrection (Cengage, 2008).

Connecticut now resided in Staten Island and were members of the famous Winthrop founders of Massachusetts. William, Robert, and Roswell were all mustered into company F, Theodore into company I. Frederick Peet Jr, son of a successful Brooklyn merchant secured a spot in company H. Albert Barrett, heir of a well-known religious leader joined Theodore Winthrop in Company I. Led by Colonel Lefferts, the Seventh did some light skirmishing duty but their term expired in June of 1861, right before the battle at Bull Run.

The war would not end there for the Seventh. In the weeks following the final muster, the Seventh contributed 70 officers to the war effort. That number would include William and Robert as Lieutenants, and Theodore as a Major, eventually joined by Barrett and Weston (Swinton, 1870). Tragically, Theodore did not make the return to trip to New York for the muster out. He volunteered to stay on as an adjutant and was the first high ranking officer killed in the war, after being shot and killed at the battle of Big Bethel. Despite the loss of manpower, the Seventh was recalled again in May of 1862 for 90 days and in June of 1863 for 90 days. In both cases the regiment was sent down to Baltimore; but was returned to New York in July of 1863 to help quell the draft riots. Their muster out of service in July of 1863 ended the war for the Seventh.

3 AUGUST 1861

Though the Seventh would provide plenty of capable leadership to other units, the Volunteer Army would still rely on the militia methods of recruiting. Through newspaper articles, Berdan sought out Crimean War veteran Caspar Trepp for a captaincy while others, like George Hastings, obtained promotions by raising a company (Berdan H. , Caspar Trepp, 1861). In state volunteer regiments this often led to incompetence at the officer level. In the sharpshooters, there was strong resentment of a major that was selected by Berdan, prompting several resignations. George Hastings, however, was careful in choosing his staff. With the training and background of Winthrop, Peet, Barrett and Weston, Hastings knew he had a solid corps of officers.

George recruited for enlisted men out of his office at 160 Montague Street in Brooklyn, and the officer staff would make trips to Long Island, upstate New York, and New Jersey when necessary. The duration of the recruiting process lasted longer than expected. The initial recruiting plan was that the Long Island Company was the second company to be raised and was therefore designated "B", but since Hastings was unable to fill a roster in time, the Albany company which was filled faster received the designation "B." Advertisements in the Brooklyn Daily Eagle show Hastings recruiting under the designation "D", however Captain George S Tuckerman[3] was able to fill his quota faster and therefore his company became "D." Once Winthrop's recruiting trip was complete the company was assigned the designation "H" (Bosley, 2010).

After signing the enlistment papers, each recruit was required to take the test. It was offered initially in Brooklyn at the target ground on the corner of Tenth Avenue and 20th Street on August 16th and 17th (Hastings G. G., For the War: Berdan's Regiment of Sharpshooters, 1861). The Long Island recruitment trip and test included stops at Babylon, Islip, Riverhead (August 27th), Sag Harbor (August 29th) and Stony Brook (August 30th). The New Jersey recruiting was done Friday, September 19th through Monday September 23rd (Local and Miscellaneous War News, 1861). Lieutenant Winthrop was detailed for a three week recruitment drive that started October 19th and was largely a Northern New York trip (Berdan H., Camp of Instruction, 1861). At that time, both Company B and Company C were busy recruiting, so Winthrop

---

[3] Tuckerman was a fellow 1851 classmate of Winthrop and Hastings at Yale. Tuckerman went north to Albany shortly after graduation, however he returned to Manhattan open offices at 51 Chambers street (Powtin, 1894).

selected a few areas which were largely untouched by other companies, including Austerlitz, Russia (Herkimer), Spencertown and Glens Falls on November 2nd (NY Daily Tribune, 1861).

As the call went out for recruits, it became apparent that Berdan's idea of a corps of sharpshooters would not come to pass. While some of the recruiters had been successful, others were not. In order to get the regiment into the field faster, some of the smaller recruiting companies were folded into the larger companies, and in some cases with poor results. Captain D.M. Brown was recruiting out of Rochester, New York for a company of Berdan Sharpshooters and like Hastings was using the newspapers to attract candidates (Berdan Sharpshooters, 1861). Unfortunately he only was successful in recruiting six men, who were sent off to Albany, to await Brown's return. When they arrived however it was a different story. They were put on a train and shipped south to join Company H. Elwood Corser, who would later become a lieutenant, EA Pratt, later captain, and four others upon learning they were assigned to Company H, instead deserted and returned to Albany. Captain Brown was sent to retrieve them, but they had already been assigned to Company B and were subsequently sent to the 93rd Infantry (Corser, 1898). In 1862 the muster rolls would be balanced with several members of Company B who were early recruits of Hastings that were sent north to Albany returned to Company H (Bosley, 2010).

Recruits began to filter in; and camps were set up at Mager's Park in

Weehawken, New Jersey, which at the time was accessible via ferry from 42nd street (NY Herald, 1861).4 This part of Weehawken was a newly formed township, only having been established in 1859. Just past the town were large expanses of open land, not yet settled, and perfect training ground.

Camp of Instruction, Weehawken, New Jersey

Company H continued to grow and train in the fields of New Jersey. New recruits arrived from New Jersey, Northern New York and Eastern Long Island. There was a bit of ebb and flow to the recruits as some were not qualified for service and were sent home before first muster. Out of the many that tried to pass the rifle test, sixteen came from Babylon expecting to enlist and ultimately only eleven would eventually muster in (Islip Corrector, 1861).5

The initial muster of 46 men occurred over a two month span starting on September 17th. Of the initial 46 all but three were recruited by Hastings himself. In the order that they were registered into the descriptive book: James Larrason, Barnard Gardner, Ezra Soper, Harvey Doolittle, Henry Smith Orrin Smith, Ebenezer Jones, John Baylis, Theodore Sands, George Wiggins, Thomas Andrews, Frederick Hartman, Charles H. Councler, John T. Schermerhorn,

---

[4] A large spacious building, the terminal would be destroyed by the 1863 draft riots, in a futile attempt to stop the army (and in part, the 7th Militia) from entering Manhattan to quell the riots.
[5] Edward Udall, whose family was quite wealthy was turned down. Additionally Joshua Taylor, P. Reilly, Henry Latting (a relative of the two Lattin boys) and William Hubbs were all turned down. Some of these men enlisted in the 127th New York instead.

Isaac Smith, and Michael McGeough all were sworn into service on the first day. Edward Barto, George Whitney, John Acker, Erastus Tooker, John J. Slifer, William Conklin, Lewis Soule followed on the next day. The initial two day muster feature a total of 15 Long Island soldiers.

William T. Edgerly, Charles Wood and Company cook, Ramsey Black, mustered in on September 23. Charles Wood, a nurse and William Edgerly were transferred out the next day. That same day seven more were mustered in: Andrew Burr, John Kenoway, Eliphalet C. Hill, William H. Lattin, John Cooley, James Campbell, and Henry Shove. Burr, Campbell, Hill and Kenoway were from Long Island. Four more were sworn in the next day including First Sergeant Albert Barrett, Lewis Strachan[6], Nathan Rouse[7], and John Fackner.

Two days later, James Thorn[8], Michael Curry, Joseph Mathews, William Seaman were sworn in followed by Jacob Crawford, Akin Ingersoll, John F. Brower[9], William Hicks, and George Lattin. The next batch of soldiers that arrived was recruited by the newly minted lieutenant Peet. This recruiting drive netted: Seth Countant, Edward Carmick, George Walters, Sylvester Lawson, Sylvester Loomis, and George Hall. With the addition of Peet's recruits, the total roster was now at 53, however shortly after arriving in camp,

---

[6] Lewis was originally in the book as Lucius A. Shackman, however his pension application and muster roll abstract has the above name used.
[7] Nathan was recruited by acting lieutenant Verplanck
[8] James was recruited by lieutenant Peet.
[9] John was recruited by acting lieutenant Verplanck

Henry Shove deserted. The next grouping of recruits was from Winthrop and included: Harvey Mathews, James Fisk, Clark Hale, John Woodard Hodgson, John Valleau, Edwin Lynde, Nicholas V. Martin, Horace Smith, Robert Helms, George Pumpelly, and Richard Boyd. According to Peet, as of November 17th, the company had 60 men on the roster, which did not include officers. His numbers were fairly accurate, as the descriptive book shows 63 (which due to Shove's desertion was actually 62).

George A Ennis was added to the roster by Harry D Tyler. George Vincent and Orrin Doty were added next, having been recruited by Henry Niles. The remainder of Tyler's recruits Thomas Williams, Henry Chasmar, John Snyder, Isaac Underhill, and Charles Ackerman followed. Unlike the rest of the top officer staff, neither Tyler nor Niles were not part of the 7th Militia clique; however both had been recruiting, Tyler in NYC and Niles near Austerlitz, under the assumption they would be given their own company should they recruit a full compliment. According to Orrin Doty's memoirs, Tyler was to be captain, Niles was to be a Lieutenant; and Doty himself a sergeant. He claimed Niles attended West Point, but there are no application papers for West Point under the name Henry Niles. Tyler and Niles were only able to recruit a total of 20, and that lead to being forced to combine with Company H (Doty O. E.). Unlike Niles and Doty, Harry D Tyler did not stay with the Sharpshooters after learning that his company would be dissolved.

After the initial half of the Tyler/Niles group was sworn in, Joseph

Hall and Charles Gruen were signed into the company register; however Charles Gruen was done so in error. He was never part of the company but will often show in roster listings due to the fact that he remained in the company descriptive book, albeit with a corrective notation. Roswell Weston, another 7th militia connection arrived into camp to be sworn in courtesy of his brother-in-law Winthrop. The remainder of the Tyler/Niles recruits was sworn in next. Levi Sabine, Niles himself, Henry Burtless, David Phelps, William Nichols, Edwin Pulver, Melanthenon Sanders, William Henry Burroughs, George Livingston, Theodore Nash, Frank Stillman, George Defendorf. The last recruit to join was Michael Mullen, although no credit was given to a recruiter. The total of the final group leaving Weehawken was 3 officers and 83 men.

1ST REGIMENT
BERDAN'S U. S.
SHARPSHOOTERS!

Lieut. Winthrop, detailed from Washington to recruit for this Regiment will

"SHOOT IN"

all who may apply, this day, in the field in rear of residence of S. Arnold Esq.

Shooting to commence at 8 o'clock, A. M. and at 2 o'clock, P. M.

Saturday, 26, Oct., 1861.

Courtesy of the Library of Congress

Albert Barrett was named first sergeant. Roswell Weston, Henry Niles and Henry Smith were the remaining sergeants. Those in the rank of corporal was reflective of the sheer number of recruits from Long Island; Jacob Crawford, Barnard Gardner and Ezra Soper from Babylon; Slifer from New York City and John T. Schermerhorn from Schenectady.

Of the initial enlistment for company H the average age for the company at muster in was 23.1 years old. This was younger than the average age of the common soldier, which were 26 according to a study done by Bell Wiley. The youngest soldiers of Company H were George Defendorf who enlisted at age 16; the oldest, were both 43, John Kenoway and Theodore Nash. The average height for Company H members was 5'7", which was a tad shorter than the average soldier height of 5'8" (Wiley, 2008). A large majority of the enlisted group had blue eyes and brown hair. Albert Barrett and George Hall were students as the war broke out, however, of the original 83, ten were carpenters, eight were clerks, three were hunters, 24 were farmers, three were machinists, two were mechanics, five were painters. Others identified as having been wickerman, tin smiths, silver smith, shoe makers, sailors or seamen, printer, japaner, cabinet maker, carman, book keeper. Levi Sabine was a physician and Issac Underhill was a druggist.

The average value of property for the enlisted man was $2,913; with George Pumpelly owning property worth $20,000, and many soldiers have property valued at $100 or less. The three officers' property average was $45,000 with George Hastings' property valued at $110,000. While most were born and lived in New York, Frederick Hartman and Charles Councler were born in Germany. William Nichols and Michael Curry were both born in Ireland; James Campbell was born in England. John Kenoway was born at sea. At least seventeen company members had ancestors that fought in a previous American war.

All told the company would enlist men from a variety of locales within New York and New Jersey however; the overwhelming majority came from Suffolk County, Brooklyn and Queens, with a total of 36 enlisted men on the books.

Equipping the Company

Hat, sergeant stripes and jacket of John T. Schermerhorn (photo courtesy Richard Smallwood-Roberts)

According to David Phelp's discharge certificate, the initial uniform outlay was $43.81 (Hastings G. G., David Phelps, 1862). In addition to the standard items that all soldiers received: socks, brogans, wool shirt, haversack, and canteen; they were also issued items very particular to the sharpshooters. The frock coat was a dark green, according to Orrin Doty's memoirs; they were almost an evergreen color (Doty O. E.). The buttons were not the standard brass buttons, they were hard rubber buttons made by the Goodyear Company; these were less reflective in the sun and aided in concealment. The "sealed" copies in the Smithsonian's collection show a lighter color on the trousers, and a forage cap in dark green as well (Smithsonian Institute, 2013).

The sharpshooters were also issued a grey overcoat and matching grey hat (called a Whipple Hat – owing to the designer) that was close enough in color to the Confederate clothing that Griffiths Battery fired into retreating sharpshooters thinking they were oncoming Rebels. Thoughts of concealment gave way to the practicality of war, and soon after, they traded the greyish overcoats for standard infantry blue overcoats and discarded the grey hats (Doty O. E.). The sharpshooters also used leather leggings and a hair-covered knapsack similar to ones issued to Prussians in Europe. Made by Tiffany & Company they were well sought after, and often disappeared if they were cast aside during battle. They were larger than standard infantry knapsacks and "fitted the back well" (Marcot, 2007). Roy Marcot had a breakdown of some of the prices of equipage in his book including: $4.25 for trousers, $3.25 for the standard blue sack coat, $2.20 for shoes, $2.15 for the knapsack (2007).

Generally during training, the army had men sleep 8 to a tent in large canvas Sibley tents. Each tent had an area for a stove, but it wasn't necessary in the summer heat. Once on the march however, the army preferred shelter tents, each soldier being issued a half. Two soldiers would combine halves at the end of the march to make a full tent. Among the group of tent mates, they would share cooking responsibilities, making sure there was always coffee available and a fire going.

The company had a cook, Ramsey Black, who was in charge of feed the regiment while in camp. While on the march men would work with their tent mates to cook meals. Orrin Smith however, did have a reputation for making a version of pancakes, whenever he had flour handy (Doty O. E.). Like many ingenious soldiers, he used a half a canteen with a split stick as a frying pan and would cook his "Panney Cakes" over the fire. Placing a tin plate behind him, he would place a cooked cake on the tin and turn back to the fire. When he was not looking the other men in the company would steal the cakes. So Orrin then spit on the cakes and said: "Now Help Yourself!"

The army issued rations of beef or pork, coffee, sugar, spices, and 9 pieces of hardtack. Food could be supplemented by foraging parties. On one such party, Orrin Doty and five others attempted to capture a malnourished pig, having to finally shoot the pig in order to catch it. In addition to the pig, they took hay and corn (Doty O. E.). Butter, eggs, and milk could be purchased through the sutlers, as could some basic necessities such as boots, shirt buttons, razors etc. (Moody, 1899). C.G. Walsh was sutler for the regiment, but in May of 1863 was accused of fraudulently absconding money that troops had paid him to obtain tickets, which could be used to purchase goods (Weston, 1863). In August of 1863, on recommendation of the officers, including Michael McGeough of company H, Ezra White was appointed sutler for the 1st Regiment of Sharpshooters (Trepp, Letter Received by the Commission Branch of the Adjutant General's Office, 1863).

Officers were expected to cloth, equip and feed themselves, however were afforded several privileges of rank. They were isolated from the mass of men, dined separately and were permitted servants as long as they were paid for by the officer. Hastings had his servant and Winthrop had brought his servant, Andy Johnson along, though Peet, often without much money could not afford to keep a servant. He did, however, keep two kittens that provided some amusement during the course of the long days (Peet F. T., Civil War Letters and Documents of Frederick Tomlinson Peet, 1917). Hastings had his own tent, Winthrop and Peet shared a tent.

The other item unique to the regiment was the Sharps Rifle. Christian Sharps, who had demonstrated the viability of the weapon to Lincoln himself, was dismayed to learn that the army felt that the men would waste too much ammunition with the breech loader. Berdan felt however it was the perfect weapon. He attempted to outfit the entire regiment at once. Sharps wouldn't be able to fill the order for several months and the sharpshooters would need to find a different weapon for the time being. To fill the void, Berdan had ordered the Colt Revolving Rifle (World, New York, 1862). The Colt Company, using the same method as with their pistol manufacturing developed a rifle that could fire several rounds before needing to be reloaded. The Sharpshooters were initially thrilled with the amount of firepower, but that soon dissipated with the major issues with the construction of the firearm being realized. Like the revolver, the musket had a tendency to fire off all the chambers at once. Keeping the revolving chambers clean while marching was difficult, and the reloading process was not easy.

Sergeants were able to carry the heavy target rifle. Just as it sounds this rifle was large, generally had a scope attached to the barrel and a small stand that would keep the barrel up when firing in a prone position. Most would land up discarding this rifle for its bulk was not worth the accuracy, and a Sharps could be just as accurate without the long reloading process of a heavy rifle.

Drill, Drill and More Drill

Life during training was anything but interesting; days were long and were spent primarily on drill. According to Regimental Order

#1: the day would run from 6:30 am through 9:10 pm. Breakfast was at 6:30 followed by sick call at 7. At 8:10 first call guard mounting occurred followed by the guard mounting at 8:15. Drill then commenced from 9:00 am until 10:15. A short break followed drill and then it was off to target practice from 10:20 am until 11:45. Dinner was at 12:00 pm and another drill was scheduled for 12:45 pm which lasted until 2:30. Soldiers were back at target practice from 3:45 until 5:00. Shortly after being recalled the first call for dress parade would be sounded near 5:15 pm. Supper was scheduled for 6:00, and the men would have off until the 9:00 tattoo and taps at 9:10.

The drills were spent studying skirmishing, a tactic the regiment would perfect during war (Marcot, 2007).

Captain Hastings was starting to earn a reputation by being strict with those who were on guard duty while he was officer of the day (Stevens, 1892). Hastings would later say that he and Casper Trepp were not well liked by the men in general, and perhaps being tough on them caused them to have this type of feeling (Hastings G. G., Letter to Lillie Devereaux , 1863). In a speech given at the dedication of the sharpshooter monument in 1889 at Gettysburg, Lt. Charles J. Buchanan stated that: "Maj George Hastings, though by nature a martinet[10], and not always popular, forced us to respect him by his bravery and gallantry" (Buchanan, 1902). Lieutenant Peet even mentioned that he would like Hastings better if the captain did not

---

[10] A martinet is a multi-tailed whip

comment on Frederick's tendency to accidentally knock things over (Peet F. T., Civil War Letters and Documents of Frederick Tomlinson Peet, 1917). Both Hastings and Trepp would issue general orders during the course of their command of the Sharpshooters that berated the regiment for sloppiness and laziness[11].

Off to Washington

Company H was ordered with the remainder of the Regiment to head down to Washington DC on November 1st. The trip down from Weehawken started with a rail transport on the New Jersey Central Railroad, to Baltimore, where they would proceed then to Washington D.C. This trip wasn't supposed to be hazardous, but riots were starting to occur more frequently in the Southern sympathizing Maryland. Lincoln quickly arrested southern sympathizers including the mayor, George William Brown, as well as the police commissioners and several others. Company H arrived in Washington DC unmolested and settled down roughly a mile from the capital on 14th and 15th Streets (Peet F. T., Personal Experiences in the Civil War, 1905). Soon, the entire regiment was there including men from Wisconsin, Vermont and Michigan.

No sooner did the company arrive and make camp then soldiers started to fall ill. Illness was a common issue in the military, as large groups of men, some not exposed to many diseases were all now closely confined and in very unsanitary conditions. The situation

---

[11] Two of Hastings regimental orders dealt with the cleanliness of weapons, one of Trepps orders dealt with laziness of sentries.

was so poor in the 1st regiment, that an Army Surgeon made several recommendations and graded the camp as unsuitable. Company D arrived in January of 1862, and soldiers upon seeing the U.S.S.S. embroidered on their captain's cap coined the phrase Unfortunately Soldiers Sadly Sold (Stevens, 1892).

The sick started in the company tents, were transferred to the regimental surgeon who would send them to the so-called Indiana Hospital for treatment. The hospital was actually the US Patent office, and the tables were set up in between the large cases which held inventions and patented items. US Army surgeons worked around the clock to deal with a variety of issues from small pox to dysentery. Others would be sent back to New York in order to recover, in many cases simply the thought was to remove the soldier from the situation in hopes their health would improve. This theory was not often successful as many would be discharged from service; however several members of Company H waited out their various ailments and would return to duty. The officers made it their responsibility to visit the sick as often as possible. Lt. Peet was a constant visitor the sick tents, and himself nearly lost a finger when it turned black and puffy (Peet F. T., Personal Experiences in the Civil War, 1905). Winthrop sent an extra person (and some whiskey) to hospital with Orrin Doty while he was recovering from the black measles (Doty O. E.). William Winthrop and George Hastings were also sick much of the time in Washington, however by January 1862, Peet had noticed that the number of illness had started to decrease (Peet F. T., Personal Experiences in the Civil

War, 1905).

For those not sick, the incessant drill continued made worse by Berdan's attempt to limit troops from heading into Washington D.C. for furlough[12]. Ebenezer Jones was caught sneaking into Washington, on November 13th and was found guilty of several counts of dereliction of duty. The courts martial sentenced him to 10 days hard labor. Boredom would only increase as the winter would limit daylight hours and the weather would limit the ability to drill.

---

[12] General order #4.

4 1862

Newly enlisted soldiers continued to flow in the camps, and Company H was bolstered by the arrival of Horace Hand and Samuel Marles, who were both late-arriving recruits of Hastings. Horace had been a teacher prior to the war, and Samuel was an artist.

Although the company added Marles and Hand, their numbers were severely reduced, as several soldiers were either discharged or still away from the company. Among those discharged: Charles Councler, Joseph Mathews and Seth Coutant all were discharged on January 10 of 1862. George Pumpelly, and Sgt. Henry C. Niles, was discharged in March. Aside from the previously mentioned illnesses, Frank Stillman, George Hall, Samuel Marles were back in New York recovering from various ailments. Later Frank Stillman and Samuel Marles deserted the army from their respective hospitals. George, who was recruited by Peet, fondly remembers

Frederick visiting him in the Patent Office Hospital. Hall would grudgingly accept being discharged, but later serve in the 14th NY Heavy Artillery (Peet F. T., Civil War Letters and Documents of Frederick Tomlinson Peet, 1917). Joseph TH Hall accepted a commission to 2nd Lieutenant of the 1st Long Island Volunteers in March of 1862. Their fighting strength of 85 enlisted would be less than 74.

It was March before the Sharpshooters were alerted for movement. Time in camp was dull and often boring. Even the most modest of soldiers would admit that they wanted time in the field, the apathy of camp could only be cured by the adrenaline that war provided. As if to inspire the troops further, they were marched past the hotel where Col. Elmer E. Ellsworth was shot and killed by the hotel owner. Col. Ellsworth had taken down the rebel flag, and the owner, a southern sympathizer shot him at point-blank range killing him[13]. The troops were also marched past the slave pens in Alexandria.

Transport ships would carry the men from Washington to Fortress Monroe on March 22nd. The officers were aboard the Emperor, the flagship for the Army's transport fleet. It was here that the Sharpshooters were exposed to their first glimpse of an ironclad and the first look at the rebel flag. For most of the men the occasion would have seemed otherworldly. Even those who had served in

---

[13] Ellsworth became a martyr for the union cause and even inspired a regiment, the 44th New York to call themselves Ellsworth's avengers.

various militias prior to the formation of the sharpshooters had not really seen any conflict. Company H was now confronted with some of the tangible evidences of war. Illness had decimated the camps, but the lives claimed had not been at the hand of an enemy, however here on Sewell Point the Rebel flag was there for all to see. They worried about the Merrimac, hearing stories about the awesome force that could destroy wooden ships with ease. When they sailed past the Monitor, Frederick Peet found it less than imposing, preferring the rebel description of a floating raft with a cheese box on top of it (Peet F. T., Civil War Letters and Documents of Frederick Tomlinson Peet, 1917). For Winthrop he was about to walk the ground where brother trod prior to his death in battle. The months of drill, endless monotony of training and regimen were about to be put to use, men would learn if they were cowards, or if they were leaders. The sharpshooters disembarked from their vessels and headed towards Hampton to establish a camp.

The Road to Yorktown

William Winthrop kept with him a copy of his brother's newly published works, which they read while encamped at Hampton waiting to make the march to Yorktown. The officers were treated to oysters and strawberries, and these last few moments exist almost as the calm before a storm. Orrin Doty told a story of how the company came across a hogshead of molasses, and all were dipping into it with their tin cups. It soon got low, and one soldier leaning too far over fell into the cask, covering himself with molasses (Doty O. E.).

While the regiment as a guide for the rest of the Union Army while on the road from Hampton to Big Bethel, it was Company H that was at the head of the column (Peet F. T., 1896). Much like the scouts and rangers of the Revolutionary War, this nimble fighting force would be able to track the enemy unseen, establish contact when necessary and hold the line until the bulk of the Army arrived. By April 4th operations were already underway to move towards Yorktown. Company H was part of the left side of the division, and was frequently thrown out as skirmishers or ordered to inspect houses and surrounding buildings (Peet F. T., 1896). They marched through mud and briars and even had sight of a few rebels at times, but largely were not bothered. The sharpshooters were able to get close enough to see the rebels put on knapsacks as they were in the process of abandoning their posts. Rather than start a skirmish when the enemy was already in flight, Company H let them leave. As they moved forward they confirmed that the rebel defensive works had been abandoned but Lt. Peet had noticed that they were quite formidable and it would have been pure slaughter if the rebels had occupied the fortification (Peet F. T., Civil War Letters and Documents of Frederick Tomlinson Peet, 1917).

The rebels did fire a few cannon shots at the advancing sharpshooters, but there was no infantry to be found anywhere. Pressing on they walked through heavy woods and roughly six miles from Yorktown, encamped (Hastings G. , 1862). The Army was stunned at the lack of defenses heading from the coast to Yorktown. What the high command staff did not realize was that there was a series of well-placed and defended batteries that ran the length of the Peninsula from the York River to the James River. On the following day, April 5th, the Sharpshooters once again pressed forward, not expecting to meet any resistance, however, they as they left the safety and security of the woods and moved towards fortifications in front of them, the Confederate batteries opened up. Company H advanced forward into the hail of bullets and cannon fire, so much so that Albert Barrett commented that their clothes were all marked with bullet holes (Stevens, 1892). They marched at the double quick to safety and they were able to harass the artillerists enough that it forced the rebels to place sandbags extra high just so that the cannons could be loaded. Once that became too dangerous, they forced the slaves to load the cannon.

Close to 4 p.m. Company H and B were placed in reserve in a hollow in the road, and were under orders not light campfires for fear of drawing attention to themselves. Despite the orders, some members from Company B lit fires and the smoke drew down fire from the batteries. The first shell was harmless; the second shell exploded overhead killing David Phelps (Peet F. T., Civil War Letters and Documents of Frederick Tomlinson Peet, 1917). According to a letter home, John Cooley was sitting near Phelps, and was the first to grab him after David was hit, Cooley, holding him in his hands as Phelps died. In addition to the death of Phelps, James Larrason was taken prisoner.

While the troops did perform admirably, Hastings was already displaying some frustration with Berdan. In a letter to Lille Devereaux, Hastings complained that a letter sent by General Porter to Berdan thanking him for the "gallant conduct and effective service" of the Sharpshooters would only increase Hiram's vanity. Hastings went further to detail some of his complaints: sending troops on useless long marches, not visiting the sick tents, being unusually harsh with the officers – especially the captains, taking all of the credit for the successful maneuvers of the troops (Hastings G. , 1862). This wouldn't be the first instance of issues with Berdan; Casper Trepp tendered his resignation in November of 1861, protesting the skills of Major Rowland and Colonel Berdan (Marcot, 2007).

The army stagnated in front of the Rebel line as McClellan waited for reinforcements and reconnaissance, assuming that the force in front of him was larger than it really was. In the days that followed Company H would send out pickets and scouts to advanced rifle pits. This was not like previous scouting or picket duty assignments. Under constant shell fire, the 20 or so men that had been assigned to the rifle pit duty were in active combat until they were relieved at night. Erastus Tooker, who was detailed as the company cook with Ramsey Black, lost a finger to a Minie ball while on duty; he was also wounded in the abdomen and leg. John Cooley referred to a duel with a black sharpshooter, where the Confederate was hiding behind a tree, and an officer with a telescopic rifle was able to shoot through a hole in the tree killing the Rebel (Murray,

2005).

Supplies were slow in getting to Company H. Many had left behind baggage and only had with them what they carried. The officers fared even worse, as they had no knapsacks in which to store items. Hastings had to borrow a blanket from his servant. The incessant rain made matters worse, and the men, taking pity on the officers built them a shanty of boards and rails (Hastings G. , 1862). The siege finally broke one month later on May 4th as a rebel deserter informed union officers that Yorktown had been abandoned. The sharpshooters charged into the fortifications to find them truly empty. Company H would rest at West Point, just north of Yorktown, and wait for the army to start on the attack again. The rebels in retreat burned their commissary stores, which resulted in a bounty for the passing sharpshooters who were able to fill their haversacks with various foodstuffs (Doty O. E.). Roswell Weston was sent to Howe's Brigade on detached service with the Quartermaster Department, he would return after the Seven Days battle.

Hanover Courthouse

The army was moving up the peninsula from Yorktown towards Richmond. The goal was still to end the war within a year. The sharpshooters were once again charged with making sure that the flanks of the advancing Union Army were protected. On May 8th, the regiments had a more secure firearm to take into battle, as now they were all equipped with the sharps breech-loading rifle.

Richmond was still a possibility and very close to advancing lines, but the Confederate Army offered a stiff resistance at the Hanover Courthouse. The battle was severely disorganized; the 44th New York received over 25% casualties during the fight. Company H arrived on the field and faced a long line of rebel troops. Once the fighting started in earnest, the sharpshooters were moved to the right for support. Upon arrival it was deemed too late for assistance and they were moved back to their original position, ending up at the extreme left. The fighting was intense, and the Confederates only withdrew once large amounts of reinforcements arrived. Roughly around this time, William Winthrop began having issues with diarrhea that became very pronounced. On June 19th, the regimental surgeon would write a report from the camp in New Bridge, asking that Winthrop be excused from duty for 30 days and be allowed to return North to recover from the ailments (Clarke, 1862).

Attrition was the fact in every war before or since the Civil War, and the effect on Company H shows the level of constant participation in battle. David Phelps was killed; Erastus Tooker, Charles Ackerman, Lewis Soule, and Horace Hand were all wounded. Two soldiers in Company B that were to be transferred into Company H: Peter Louis and Clinton Loveridge[14] were both

---

[14] Clinton Loveridge was wounded so badly his leg needed to be amputated (Albany Evening Journal, 1862). Already somewhat famous before the war as an artist, rather than be discharged, Clinton accepted a transfer and promotion to Lieutenant in the Veteran Reserve Corps, which was designated to handle paperwork and desk type duties.

wounded as well. Theodore Nash, Ebenezer Jones, Lewis Strachan, and Melanethon Sanders, George Ennis, Samuel Marles, George F. Hall, William Winthrop, John Fackner, Henry Chasmar, Frederick Hartman, George Defendorf and Charles Ackerman were all sick and away from the regiment. On June 20th, Andrew Burr was wounded, and would be discharged later in the year. Despite heavy losses during the month of May, Company H and the 1st US Sharpshooters had acquitted themselves very well thus far and were considered to be an effective and useful fighting force.

Seven Days Battle

McClellan aware that Stonewall Jackson was lurking on his flank, and knowing that if he were to win a decisive victory it would have to be before Jackson was able to take the field, ordered his army forward.

Company H was detached from the Regiment and ordered to General Sumner. He assigned Hastings and Company H to assist Richardson's Division. Hastings counted his command on the way to the assignment and logged 39 soldiers, including himself and Lt. Peet. Peet was ill, but remained with the company.

Hastings, who was already soured on Berdan's command, was thrilled to be on his own. With Hastings acting as commanding officer of the independent company, the sharpshooters were given difficult and dangerous assignments. In one case Albert Barrett was sent to the Nine-Mile Road to stop Confederate harassment of the

Union picket line. Taking three other sharpshooters, Barrett rigged up a stick with a hat and a coat and waited for the Rebel to fire. Once he did, the sharpshooters were able to hone in on the tree from where the shot came from and silenced the Confederate (Stevens, 1892).

The Seven Days Battle started on June 25th with fighting near Oak Grove. Company H would not be involved in any heavy action immediately, however, every day consisted of dangerous picket duty or worse, reconnoitering the front. Horace Smith, who was just promoted to corporal, would be wounded at Gaines Mill. John Cooley who had been out sick volunteered to go with Company D on skirmish duty (Murray, 2005).

Company H was on picket duty during the 28th and 29th, and as the army retreated from Oak Grove, they had neglected to inform Company H. Hastings upon recall of his company found everyone else had left except one battery, and now Company H was the closest Union unit to Richmond, and all by themselves. During the retreat they could hear yells from Confederate forces, which had discovered the abandon Union position. Hastings had Company H take to the woods in order to hide their retreat and rejoin with the army (Stevens, 1892). Still protecting the retreat towards the river, Captain Hastings received orders to throw out the company as skirmishers so as to be able to fire on the road from the Chickahominy.

Hastings was given a small command of cavalry, two companies of infantry, one artillery piece, a hospital wagon and a transport wagon (Hastings G. G., Letter to Lillie Devereaux, 1862). Hastings spread out along the tree line facing an open field, and the company could see movement in the tree line; however it was only pockets of men, not an entire body of an army. Hastings knew that firing on random targets may bring a response that would overpower the sharpshooters; he reported to headquarters that the enemy in front was not in force. The main portion of the federal army in that area was starting to divert to Savage Station. By this time the adrenaline had flown through the men's veins for several long hours, even though there was no firing and no fighting, it was intolerably hot and they were exhausted (Hastings, #114, 1862). Hastings had orders to relax and regroup in the shade while at Savage Station and this provided some much needed rest for the men. There was no fighting during the night; however the army moved through the White Oak Swamp, which was a slow process and lasted much of that night into next morning.

Hastings was unable to locate a General for orders so he formed up next to General Caldwell's brigade during the morning which was situated near the center of the Union line, just north of Glendale. Since he had not received any orders, and since they were already in Caldwell's Brigade, Hastings opted to report to Colonel Barlow[15] of the 61st NY for the day, and spent the afternoon ensuring that the batteries were protected from Rebel probing. From the moment that

---

[15] Francis Barlow was also a Harvard Alumni graduating in 1855.

Company H entered into battle on the 30th they were under constant fire. The artillery had opened up to disrupt the supply chain of pontoon boats, and they were largely successful as the firing was able to get the mules who were hauling the boats to stampede. The Union army decided to burn the boats rather than have them fall into enemy hands.

The shells rained down on the company continuously, one shell landing in between Hastings and Albert Barrett's head. At this point, Hastings servant who was loaded down with his blankets, haversack and other items said "Dis is no place for me, sar" and took off with Hastings' personal items, never to be seen again (Stevens, 1892). Another shell landed in between John Acker and Edward Lynde, and it tore the blanket roll off of Lynde's shoulder. Counter-battery action from the rebels kept the 61st and Company H pinned against a mound until roughly 6:30 in the evening.

Col. Meagher of the famous Irish brigade ordered Barlow in to a wooded area on their way towards the James River. Hastings under orders from Barlow occupied the right flank of the 61st and was placed in command of the wing. Lt. Peet assumed Winthrop's duties for this battle. They had crossed from the road towards an open field; on the double quick. Hastings estimates that nearly a third of his men collapsed from fatigue (Hastings G. G., Letter to Lillie Devereaux, 1862). Down to twenty five men, and pressing on towards the rebel position, Lt. Peet saw Col. Barlow had picked up a rebel flag and urged his men forward. Directly in front of them was a wooded area, and just beyond that, a stone fence. Once into the woods it had turned to dusk and was very difficult to make out friend from foe. A voice called out asking what regiment they were, and Hastings replied that it was the 61st NY. The rebel asked for a surrender and threatened to "blow them all to hell" if they did not comply (Peet F. T., Personal Experiences in the Civil War, 1905). Barlow ordered the men to duck as the rebels opened up. The musketry was overwhelming but the Union forces were able to start returning fire. Almost immediately Lt. Peet, who was trying to assess the situation, was shot, and collapsed unconscious. Sgt. John Slifer was lying down and was shot in the back and wrist, Richard Boyd and Woodard Hodgson were both shot in head, Sylvester Lawson was shot in the foot, and both Edward Lynde and John Valleau were both shot in the hip.

When Peet came to, he saw what was left of his side of the company firing away; he called out for help and was taken back to the field hospital along with Slifer, Valleau and Lawson. The remainder was able to stay with the company as they retreated. Hastings saw his lieutenant at the field hospital as the company marched past, Peet felt that he was probably not going to make it through the night, and asked that Hastings tell his mother that he loved her[16]. In a show of devotion to their beloved officer, both private Martin Nichols and private Edward Carmick offered to stay with Peet to keep him safe (Hastings G. G., Letter to Lillie Devereaux, 1862). As

---

[16] The doctors warned Peet that due to the placement of the bullet if he coughed, he would probably die. They wanted to amputate his arm, but Peet refused.

was expected the rebels overtook the hospital later that night and captured Peet, Carmick, Nichols, Valleau, Lawson and Slifer.

Company H effectively stopped being a company. Captain Hastings, after his trip to see Peet at the hospital was unable to locate but two of his men. Some had assisted their comrades to the hospital; others had collapsed from fatigue during the double quick march. John Cooley and John Schermerhorn had volunteered with Company C just before the battle started and fought with Regimental Adjutant John Smith Brown. They had held the rebels off for five hours before the Irish Brigade charged and pushed the rebels back. Cooley was so exhausted that he could not catch up with Company H (Murray, 2005).

Hastings offered himself up as a Lieutenant for Barlow and served in that role before being moved to Caldwell's Aide (Hastings G. G., Letter to Lillie Devereaux, 1862). During the normal course of his duties, he located some Sharpshooters from Company B that were formed in a wooded area, and moved them into line with Caldwell. It was not until Harrison's Point on July 3rd that Hastings caught up with what remained of Company H. There were 28 men left, on paper, but all that Captain Hastings took with him when they returned to Richardson's division was 15.

Four remained with the regiment too sick to join them. Orrin Doty was sent to a Philadelphia hospital to recover from dysentery, he would return in time for Antietam. Doty attributed his recovery to some pickled string beans provided by Winthrop's cook Andy

Johnson (Doty O. E.). Also sent to General Hospitals were: John Baylis, Horace Smith, James Campbell, William Conklin, Robert Helms, George Livingston, Levi Sabin, John Snyder, Frank Stillman, Thomas Williams and George Vincent. Still not returned were William Winthrop and George Ennis. In addition the Sharpshooter leadership was in disarray: Berdan was convalescing, Lt. Col Ripley was severely wounded, and Capt. Drew, one of the better officers, was killed, and with several other officers wounded.

On July 18th the Company H privates that were taken captive with Peet were exchanged for Southern prisoners (New York Tribune, 1862)[17]. Eventually Carmick, Nichols and Lawson would return to rejoin the company. Peet would miraculously survive the wound and accept the offered position of 2nd Lieutenant in the Marine Corps. During the course of the action on the 30th Henry Burtless a farmer from Seneca Falls before the war, would desert. John T. Schermerhorn who would later act as 1st Sgt for Company H wrote home that of the 80 men who would enter into battle with Company H, only 18 would walk out of the Seven Days Battle unscathed. The company, especially the leadership had been decimated. John Cooley stated that he did not care if he was taken prisoner or if he were killed, he was so disgusted with the war and with destruction (Murray, 2005). He wrote in a different letter that "I have seen men lay on the ground crazy with the typhoid fever, in the cold rain, in the mud and water, no one to take care of them and there are

---

[17] Only Peet and Nichols were listed

thousands of such. I do not know whether it is right or not. You will hear tales of horror that I dare not write, through other sources."

Albert Barrett would finally get his promotion, but not in company H (Porter F. J., 1862). While very common in the modern army to transfer out of the company once promoted from non-commissioned to a commissioned rank it was not as common during the Civil War. In fact several promotions would occur within Company H as wounds, illness and promotions depleted the officer ranks. Albert, most likely noted that a lesser sergeant in Roswell Weston had favored status within the command of Company H and that it would make sense that since Frederick Peet was leaving there should have been an open spot. Barrett, however would instead take a different opportunity, in late May Horace Chase, a second lieutenant with company D had resigned his commission. Albert Barrett transferred over and took Chase's spot and Roswell Weston gained a commission and took Frederick Peet's position as second lieutenant. Albert would be discharged a month later.

The sergeant staff was missing Slifer, Niles and Henry Smith. Henry Smith was ill, and would be discharged in September from the Newport News Hospital. In turn John T. Schermerhorn and Barnard Gardiner would be promoted to sergeant. And Slifer, though captured was made 1st Sergeant.

Hastings was hoping to get a furlough home, but with no Lieutenants on staff, he would be forced to wait. Experiencing independent command himself and proving that he was capable of leading troops, he did not want to return to Berdan's Regiment if Berdan was still in charge. Hastings confided to Lillie Devereaux that he was worried he may himself be a coward, but was glad to see that he was not. However he preferred resignation to serving with Berdan.

In the months between the end of the Seven Days and the start of the Second Bull Run three members of company H died from disease: Joseph Newberry on July 30th, George Vincent on August 8th and Ramsey Black on August 20th.

Second Bull Run

What remained of the Company limped towards Malvern Hill, but would be spared having to fight. The disaster of the Peninsula Campaign cost McClellan his position as the top ranking general in the Union army. Henry Halleck was promoted to McClellan's vacant spot, and for the remainder of July and August, consolidated his forces. McClellan stayed as the commander of the Army of the Potomac. The Confederate Army wanted to boost morale and continue pressure on Union forces. Robert E. Lee, commanding the rebels since the Seven Days Battles, began pressure northward. Believing that he had sprung a trap, General Pope focused a concentrated assault on Stonewall Jackson's army. The casualties were horrific, and not realizing that Longstreet had arrived with his corps, Pope continued to assault Jackson's position. On the extreme right flank of the Union Army, the Berdans were advancing as skirmishers in front of General Butterfield's division.

The regiment had not seen much action the first day; however on the second day, August 30th, they had cleared a section of woods and found themselves facing a large Confederate force. Berdan was ordered to push his men through the woods, but had refused on the account that it would have been suicidal. When support did finally arrive, the sharpshooters went ahead skirmishing, though casualties would be severe. Company H held the position and did not flee as others had. Hastings, Winthrop and Weston along with six other sharpshooters were the last to the leave the field, and they did so carrying wounded soldiers (Hastings G. G., Letter to Lillie Devereaux, 1862). William Lattin and George Whitney were wounded. George Barber, another Company B member that would later be transferred into Company H was wounded as well. Lattin would be transferred to the invalid corps as a result of his wounds and George Barber would receive an outright discharge for the wound in his leg (New York, Town Clerks' Registers of Men Who Served in the Civil War, ca 1861-1865). George Whitney would heal and return to duty. Second Bull Run would be a colossal failure for Pope, he would be relieved of command and his forces merged with the Army of Potomac under McClellan.

As time passed in 1862, the outlook for Company H did not get any better, after Bull Run they were afforded a short opportunity to rest from three straight months of combat. Private's Carmick and Nichols were returned to the ranks after being released from Libby Prison. Winthrop returned to the regiment on assignment. John Cooley[18], Clark Hale and Orrin B. Smith[19] would be discharged before the next campaign. George Hastings would be taken from the Company and promoted to acting Major, thanks in part to recommendation from Richardson (Hastings G. G., Letter to Lillie Devereaux, 1862). This created a ripple effect in the officer staff, Winthrop was promoted to during the Maryland Campaign to Captain, Weston to first Lieutenant. Michael McGeough was promoted to 2nd Lieutenant, bypassing John Slifer.

The company strength before the start of the summer campaigns was at 74 enlisted. The roster at the end of the Second Bull Run was only 57 names. Samuel Marles, Frank Stillman and Henry Burtless had deserted. Harvey Doolittle was discharged in April, Theodore Nash in May. Ebenezer Jones, Horace Hand, Lewis Strachan, Melanethon Sanders and Erastus Tooker were all discharged in June. Clark Hale and John Cooley were discharged in July, Orrin Smith in August. Frederick Peet had resigned and Albert Barrett along with Jospeh Hall had been transferred. David Phelps, George Vincent and Ramsey Black were all dead. Not counting those away sick, the initial roster of 88 had suffered three deaths, four desertions, 16 discharges, four transfers, and two enlisted taken from the ranks to serve as officers.

---

[18] John Cooley would be asked to train 148th NY Volunteers and eventually be promoted to major. Post-war Cooley was commissioned a 2nd Lieutenant in the regular infantry, serving with the 13th.

[19] Orrin B. Smith would eventually join the US Navy and serve for the remainder of the war.

Antietam

The 1st US Sharpshooters were severely crippled entering September of 1862. Hastings estimated that the original strength of 900 was now down to roughly 200 (Hastings G. G., Letter to Lillie Devereaux, 1862). A combination of disease, wounds, desertions and discharges left the sharpshooters severely undermanned.

Lee, knowing that the Union Army was again changing command, took an opportunity to invade northward. Knowing that Maryland had southern sympathies, Lee took the initiative to move towards Washington. In a bold stroke he divided his forces to attack the Union troops that were backed into Sharpsburg, Maryland. The sharpshooters in the first regiment were held in reserve and under heavy fire throughout the battle of Antietam.

Following the battle, Company H and several other units followed the remainder of the Confederate Army in an attempt to stop them from escaping. The Sharpshooters caught up with the rebels roughly a mile downstream from Shepherdstown, West Virginia, where there is a ford in the Potomac River. Called by several names, Blackford's Ford provided an easy crossing for Confederate forces to head back into Virginia. General Fitz-John Porter noted in his report on the battle that the Confederates had fortified the banks of the ford with artillery and had posted the sharpshooters along with skirmishers in an attempt to capture the Confederate artillery (Porter F.-J., 1887).

After the battle of Antietam, there were only 225 men left in the 1st Regiment of Sharpshooters, down from 1000 in 1861 (Murray, 2005). Berdan himself was away on leave recruiting, which would bring the regimental strength up to 500. Trepp in the meantime was in charge of the regiment, and Hastings expressed a good working relationship with the Lieutenant Colonel (Hastings G. G., Letter to Lille Devereaux, 1862). In a letter to the Adjutant General of the V Corps, Trepp related the strength of the company at enlistment was 72, and currently was at 47 (Marcot, 2007).

With nearly all the regimental officers either wounded or assigned, Captain Isler of Company A was put in charge of the Regiment. The sharpshooters, after skirmishing, were ordered to advance across the ford by Colonel Barnes. With only a portion of the line hearing the command to move forward, Winthrop along with Lieutenant William Nash of Company B and roughly 60 men crossed the ford. Winthrop led the line and was the first to step on Virginia soil. They were able to capture one prisoner who identified the rebels as belonging to General Hood, shortly after they re-crossed and camped for the evening (Isler, 1889).

The next day the Sharpshooters provided covering fire for an assault by fresh troops. Being turned back by Stonewall Jackson, Winthrop again crossed the ford to assist troops getting back across the river (Kastenberg, 2009). Following the battle the army moved down the Potomac through Harper's Ferry, down through Louden Valley stopping at the Blue Ridge Mountains.

Shortly after the battle ended, Orrin Doty on picket duty saw a horse coming out of the darkness at him. In a panic he shouted then fired his weapon, but nothing happened. From behind him a distraught Major Hastings yelled for him not to shoot his horse. Hastings had fallen asleep and his horse had decided to walk down the mountain (Doty O. E.). Hastings complained of problems with transporting company and regimental supplies again following the march through Harper's Ferry. With the weather turning cold, soldiers had to attempt to sleep as close to a fire as possible or risk freezing yet at the same time try to avoid the smoke.

As they approached Snickers Gap on the Blue Ridge, snipers from a house began firing at the sharpshooters. Winthrop, with sword drawn entered the house searching for the snipers but managed only to locate the women and eventually after using his sword to search bedding and clothes found one male, who could not or would not give further information (Hastings G. G., Letter to Lille Devereaux, 1862). The sharpshooters ate breakfast and paid the owner of the house for two chickens.

During the course of the Maryland Campaign there was an ebb and flow to Company H's roster. Robert Helmes, George Defendorf, John Baylis and Henry Smith were discharged in September. Andrew Burr, Frederick Hartman, Henry Chasmar, Edward Barto, George Hall and George Walters would follow in October.

Noah Olds, would be the 90th recruit for Company H, arriving in early September. John Wilson, Lieutenant of Company B, and friend of Hastings prior to the war, had spent time recruiting with Berdan prior to Antietam, and netted several recruits for Company H. Marvin Hildabrant, William Haggart, John Chambers, George Simmons, John Bela, Henry Ecker, Aaron Fuller, Philip Service, Joseph Newberry, and George Countryman were all added to the muster roll. The Company B transfers of William Gillian, Patrick Joyce, Peter Louis, Clinton Loveridge, George Barber and Richard Foster were completed before the battle of Fredericksburg.

Andrew Westervelt, who had lived in California and worked as a miner, would last recruit of Company H to be in the book[20]. Andrew moved back east after the start of the war. Selling off all of his property in California, he donated the sum to the government. His friends raised funds for him to head east and join a regiment to fight. He enlisted along with, Truman Head, famously nicknamed California Joe. They were both personally recruited by Berdan.

Fredericksburg

Following Maryland Campaign the armies prepared to make winter camp. Moral in the army was starting to shrink, Company H was no exception. Twice Hastings had to issue orders related to keeping weapons clean. General Order #5 stated that any offender found to have unclean weapons is to be punished and reported to headquarters. He followed that with Regimental Order #8 stating that the rifles are frequently rusty and dirty and that company

---

[20] Charles Hicks joined the company in 1863, though was never written into the descriptive book.

officers should take pride in their men, rifles and accoutrements and therefore anyone who has a dirty weapon needs to be punished (Skillman, Carey, & White, Who were they? The 1st Regiment U.S. Sharpshooter Armorers, 2012).

The sharpshooters did not partake in any of the assaults at Fredericksburg, however Major Hastings took four companies out to skirmish, including Company H, and they were spread out in a line between General Franklin's right flank and the railroad (Trepp, Report of Lieutenant Colonel Casper Trepp, First US Sharpshooter, 1862). Company H watched as the army made charge after suicidal charge, and was baffled that Halleck, Burnside and Stanton were all still firmly entrenched in their positions (Peet F. T., Civil War Letters and Documents of Frederick Tomlinson Peet, 1917)[21]. Following the battle, and perhaps realizing the value of having long range target rifles to disrupt officers and artillery, Berdan sent Captain Winthrop to Washington to attempt to find the target rifles that had been turned in during 1861. They had been scattered, and Winthrop was under orders to select the best possible rifles to bring back (Berdan H. , Camp Near Falmouth VA, 1862).

Company H, along with the rest of the sharpshooters marched from Fredericksburg to their winter homes in Falmouth. Unfortunately this would not end the fighting for the year for Company H.

---

[21] Hastings and Winthrop would make similar comments in separate letters to Frederick Peet, now with the Marine Corps. Moral was flagging and neither were impressed with the Army's leadership or the representation of the troop's moral in the newspapers.

Skirmishing along the Rappahannock with Confederate Calvary on New Year's Eve, Hastings had a brigade of three companies; B,G and H. They forded the river at Richard's Ford and marched six miles to Ellis Ford. Sylvester Lawson, Noah Olds and Andrew Westerverlt were able to get a prisoner and brought a sword and pistol to Captain Winthrop.

Winthrop complained that his boots were soaked through and spent the New Year drying them out (Peet F. T., Civil War Letters and Documents of Frederick Tomlinson Peet, 1917). In order for the boots to come off, several men had to pull on them, knocking him over and the water spilled onto his face (Doty O. E.). John Schermerhorn complained that fording the river twice in water up to his chest left him cold hungry and tired, but he did manage to capture a chicken on the way back and was able to roast it for a nice dinner (Murray, 2005).

As Company H settled into Camp Falmouth, the ranks would be further diminished. In some cases it was merely book keeping as many of these soldiers had not been with the company for several months. The following were discharged: George Ennis, Charles Ackerman, William Haggart, James Campbell, John Kenoway, John Fackner, Levi Sabine, George Barber, George Crawford, Edwin Pulver, John Chambers, and John Valleau. Although he would stay on the Company H muster roll, Winthrop would be in Washington for the majority of the remainder of the war. Nathaniel Rouse would not be as lucky, and he would die from disease on Christmas

Eve. George Hastings spent Christmas Eve at Brown's Hotel with Lillie Devereaux (Hastings G. G., Letter to Lillie Devereaux, 1862). On a positive note, Roswell Weston was due back to the regiment after the New Year (Peet F. T., Civil War Letters and Documents of Frederick Tomlinson Peet, 1917).

The descriptive book for Company H had been filled with 108 names. Of those Gruen never served, two were promoted out of the ranks and 50 were no longer with the company. The roster though bolstered with replacements stood at a mere 55. Having physical bodies in the ranks was one issue; moral of those that remained was another.

Just after Christmas, Caspar Trepp, much beloved by the troops for having all the qualities in a leader that Berdan was lacking attempted to resign after he and Hastings were ordered to perform the manual of arms, being instructed by a lieutenant. Even though this was as bad an insult that a commanding officer can receive, both Hastings and Trepp participated in the drill. The discontent that Trepp, Hastings and Winthrop had for Berdan only intensified after this, and created a situation that was destroying the cohesive bonds needed to function as an effective unit.

5 1863

The sharpshooters had a real opportunity to rest and refit at the beginning of the year. Winter quarters were constructed at Falmouth, Virginia, and after the disaster at Fredericksburg, it was assured the army would not be making any bold moves. Even though it was a period of rest, nothing was at peace in the first regiment. The contempt and scorn that Trepp, Hastings and Winthrop felt for him would be amplified due to his intentionally offensive orders. In turn Berdan had been accused of cowardice at Gaines Mill and again at Chickahominy which resulted in a recommendation for promotion to Brigadier General was withdrawn[22].

As this battle between the high command of the 1st Sharpshooters intensified, Berdan took the only step he felt was left, and attempted to rid the Sharpshooters of what he felt were the trouble makers. Trepp, Winthrop and Hastings were all jailed by Berdan to await a

---

[22] General Porter withdrew his recommendation citing he did not have faith in his abilities and did not want to place him in command of so many lives.

courts martial.

Trepp was arrested for stealing stationary, and cowardice. He was defended by Colonel Strong Vincent[23]. Many officers provided willing testimony for Trepp and his charges were eventually dismissed (Kastenberg, 2009).

Winthrop was arrested on January 25th for conduct unbecoming an officer when a private overheard Winthrop say to Trepp: "If I were in your place I would not obey Col. Berdan's orders and I advise you not to." On February 6th Winthrop sent a letter to Berdan indicating that by military law, he should have been brought to trial within 10 days, and at this moment he had already surpassed the 12 day mark (Winthrop, Camp near Falmouth VA, 1863). Winthrop was questioned by General Whipple in regards to the statement, which Berdan then asked Winthrop to compose a written statement in regards to the charges against him. Winthrop responded in a letter dated February 18th to Berdan that military law required no such statement to be provided to him (Winthrop, Camp Near Falmouth , 1863). On February 19th Berdan acquiesced and released Winthrop stating that there was some confusion about the order that Wintrop suggested Trepp disobeys. This event would lead to Winthrop's general dissatisfaction with the rules regarding courts martials and the rights of the soldiers being held. He would make it a life mission to attempt to perfect the legal system in the army.

---

[23] A hero of Gettysburg, Col. Vincent would die at Little Round Top.

Hastings was arrested initially for stealing stationary. Ultimately, Hastings was also charged with conduct unbecoming an officer, with the specifications of: disobeying direct orders, and three counts all related to insults of Berdan that were overheard in many cases by his friend Captain Wilson. As a lawyer Hastings prepared his own defense while he waited out the time until the courts martial.

Before the Hastings trial could commence, Berdan then had the tables turned on him, and charges were filed. Hastings was ready to testify that Berdan had lied to the inspector general about receiving bayonets with the sharps rifle (Marcot, 2007). Because Berdan was arrested, the Hastings trial could not go forward in the timeframe set forth by Article 79, though in a letter to Lillie Devereaux, he almost makes it seem as if he prefers it (1863). Hastings hoped that this meant an end to Berdan as leader of the sharpshooters, and all of the "sycophants" who were detailed to Berdan's staff would be returned to their regiment (Hastings G. G., Letter to Lillie Devereaux, 1863).

Winthrop was transferred out of the company on a temporary basis starting on March 10th when he was ordered by General Bartlett to special duty on his staff[24]. Winthrop would not return to the regiment but remained on the roster, as all of the assignments to various JAG duties were considered temporary in nature[25].

---

[24] Special order 68

[25] Disgusted with the courts martial process and Berdan himself, Winthrop made a career out of military justice, teaching Military Law at West Point, and writing several books in regards to military law, some of which are still in use today.

As sure as the officer moral was lagging, the enlisted men would take their cues from their commanding officers. The more angry and upset the leaders were, the soldiers became so too. Slifer, who had just been promoted to first sergeant, Issac Underhill and Richard Foster all deserted in the months leading to Chancellorsville. After Chancellorsville, George Campbell would desert. Following Gettysburg, Michael Mullin, Patrick Joyce, William Seaman and Theodore Sands would desert; Akin Ingersoll[26] deserted on New Year's Eve.

The army tracked desertions during the Civil War, but it was not an exact science. Lewis Soule, for example, was thought to be a deserter at the Wilderness, when in reality he had been captured. A thorough accounting of desertions done in 1928 showed the Union army had roughly 200,000 desertions, the most coming when moral was low. The total number accounted for roughly 8% of all enlisted soldiers (Lonn, 1928). Company H, however, had an unusually high rate of desertions, 15%. The nine desertions of 1863 reflect the attitudes of the soldiers, who had lost faith in their leadership, questioned the war effort and had seen so many of their comrades become casualties. It became so bad during 1863 that Hastings had to return north to attempt to find at least the soldiers who had deserted from hospitals and furloughs. Of the 13 total deserters from Company H, five had been recruited by Hastings, three by Tyler, three were from Company B, one who was recruited by Peet,

---

[26] Akin would return and serve the remainder of the war with Company H.

and Mullen who had no recruiter listed.

The morale for the army was no better. As they had expected, Burnside was eventually replaced, but not by McClellan, whom they had hoped for, but by Joe Hooker, who had a reputation for aggressiveness, prostitutes and alcohol. Prior to the battle of Chancellorsville, there was a series of promotions to fill the depleted ranks. John T. Schermerhorn was promoted to first sergeant to replace the Slifer. Horace Smith and Edward Carmick were promoted to sergeant. John Acker and James Fisk were promoted to corporal. Additionally others were discharged: George H Countryman from the convalescent camp, Thomas Williams from Alexandria, James Larrason from Davis Island, and John Bala.

Chancellorsville

Berdan, once again in control of his brigade of sharpshooters spent much of the first day at Chancellorsville skirmishing (Berdan, #149, 1863). No one had known that at the time the 11th Corps was being routed, nor were they immediately aware that Stonewall Jackson, after nearly breaking the back of the Union Army had been killed in an instance of friendly fire. The next day, the 3rd, was one of the toughest fought days of that battle.

The 124th New York came across the sharpshooters, commanded by Major Hastings in a thick wood. The rebels began firing on the front and right flank, but the 124th and the sharpshooters, who were ordered to protect a battery, held fast (Ellis A. V., 1863). Doty and one of the lieutenants were hiding behind trees when the shelling started, as they started to retreat, they ran into each other, falling down a hill (Doty O. E.)., Major Hastings had three horses shot out from under him, and was severely wounded in the knee (Stevens, 1892). Hastings attempted to play down the nature of his wound telling Peet it was not serious and in fact he was on his way back to New York (Peet F. T., Civil War Letters and Documents of Frederick Tomlinson Peet, 1917). He also wrote a letter to Lillie Devereaux telling her not to worry. He claimed the wound was a "jolly circumstance" (Hastings G. G., Letter to Lillie Devereaux, 1863). In June George sent a piece of his coat with the bullet hole to Lillie Devereaux. The wound however did prevent him from returning to the regiment and may have led to his early death in 1873. Joseph Hooker in his report to award Hastings with the rank of brevet Lt. Colonel wrote that the skirmish line of the sharpshooters was attacked from left to right by full regiments of Confederates, all which were repulsed by the skirmishers. Hooker also noted that Hastings had already been twice cited for bravery, once at Malvern Hill and once at Second Bull Run (Hooker, 1866)[27].

Heading into Gettysburg, on paper, the company had 52 soldiers left. William Lattin, Richard Boyd, and Clinton Loveridge were all severely injured and would eventually be transferred to the invalid corps. Joseph Newberry was sick with typhus in Annapolis,

---

[27] Hastings and Winthrop along with several other officers would rent an apartment in Washington at 255 H St. for remainder of the war (Peet F. T., Civil War Letters and Documents of Frederick Tomlinson Peet, 1917).

Maryland. Winthrop was out of the company assigned to the Judge Advocates. Roswell Weston was serving as an adjutant with the regiment since February, leaving the company with Michael McGeough as the only officer. George Hastings returned to New York, and began rounding up troops that had been on furlough. On June 23 he headed to Islip to attempt to find some of the Babylon troops that had returned home and had not come back to the company. Afterwards he returned to the Willard's Hotel in Washington (Hastings G. G., Letter to Lillie Devereaux , 1863).

Gettysburg

Leaving Chancellorsville, Company H, part of the Third Corps marched from Middletown Maryland, on through Frederick Maryland, and Walkersville ending in Emmetsburg. The division occupied the road heading toward Taneytown that leads north into Gettysburg (Birney, #133, 1863). On July 2nd, Company H, along with the rest of the 1st and 2nd Regiments of Sharpshooters were in the peach orchard on the Millerstown Road. Berdan received orders to send 100 sharpshooters into the woods to reconnaissance the position of the Confederate Army. Company H and company B, with Casper Trepp in charge temporarily, they were in the woods from roughly 7:30 in the morning until 5:00 in the evening skirmishing with the enemy, until all ammunition was expended, and a heavy Rebel force pushed them back. A second group of 100 sharpshooters was requested at 11:00 am further down the road. Casper Trepp turned over command of the first 100 sharpshooters to Captain John Wilson and took command of the second group. They located three enemy columns attempting to change direction. This group was able to keep the Confederates occupied for three hours. Under the immediate command of Captain Baker, the First Regiment moved to the right of the peach orchard and attempted to keep the Confederates at bay. Captain Baker led a charge across the field driving the Rebels away. During this skirmish, Casper Trepp called attention out specifically to Martin V. Nichols and William H. Nichols for their bravery (Trepp, #150, 1863). The morning of the July 3rd the Sharpshooters were moved to the 6th Corps, who were fighting generally on the eastern side of Gettysburg. On July 4th, the Regiment was sent briefly out as pickets, and later 100 volunteers from Companies H, B, G and D more were asked to reconnaissance in force, but without results (Murray, 2005). During the course of the battle, Barnard Gardiner was wounded, John T Schermerhorn would be so badly wounded yet, after superior officers attempted to discharge him, he refused to go (Stevens, 1892). Noah Olds, who was mentioned in several reports for bravery was wounded in the right thigh.

Following Gettysburg, the Army offered little pursuit of the Confederates, either they were too afraid of another assault into Pennsylvania, or distracted by rioting in New York, or simply by being exhausted emotionally and physically from the toll that Gettysburg placed on the army. This allowed for some time to regroup for the sharpshooters. They were reissued clothing to replace worn down uniforms. In a paper in 2002, Berdan expert Bill Skillman theorized that during the campaign, the green coats had been traded in for blue blouses. This would account for why four blouses needed replacing, and why no green coats were requested. Overall, Company H received four coats, 13 shirts, 4 pairs of drawers, 27 pairs of socks, 1 hat, 16 pairs of shoes and 10 pairs of pants. Of the 10 pairs of pants, three were for a size 32 waist, six for a size 34 and one for a size 36. In regards to the shoes, one wore a size 5, one a size 6, three a size 7, seven a size 8, three a size 9 and one a size 10. For equipment, Company H requested 11 haversacks, 9 canteens, 11 blankets and 6 tents (Skillman, What did they Wear? A post-Gettysburg analysis of Clothing and Equipment requisitioned by the 1st USSS on July 28, 1863., 2002).

Company H lost their commanding officer as Roswell Weston was sent to New York in September of 1863 having been horribly disfigured by an attack of scurvy. It was so bad that Winthrop having passed him on the streets of Washington did not recognize him (Peet F. T., Civil War Letters and Documents of Frederick Tomlinson Peet, 1917). Hastings made an attempt to rejoin the sharpshooters in late July, again complaining of the lack of supply wagons and having to sleep out in the elements, however supporting Meade in that a follow-up attack after Gettysburg would have been foolish (Hastings G. G., Letter to Lillie Devereaux, 1863). Additionally Michael Curry was sent to Culpepper ill. In October to fill depleted ranks, Eliphalet Hill was promoted to sergeant. By

September, Hastings had returned to the Judge Advocate Generals and was living with Winthrop, although he preferred to return to the Sharpshooters, so long as Berdan was not in command. Hastings and Winthrop were going to be assigned to Washington as long as there were court martials to be conducted. In truth Hastings did not mind the work, and would seek a judge advocate position with an army in the field (Hastings G. G., Letter to Lillie Devereaux, 1863).

Mine Run

Casper Trepp was now in full command of the 1st US Sharpshooters had guided them through the Second Battle of the Rappahannock without much issue. On the move to strike Lee through the wilderness, the army ran into trouble trying to get artillery, ambulances and wagons up the bluff opposite Jacob's Mills. As a result the force was diverted to Germanna Ford, which allowed Lee to react (Birney, #44, 1863). The sharpshooters were involved Tuesday the 26th of November in picket duty with Third Brigade, supporting the 17th Maine, 68th Pennsylvania, 3rd and 5th Michigan and the 40th New York. They held a position skirmishing with the enemy throughout the day on the 27th. During the course of the action, James Fisk was shot in the head. The sharpshooters were used to reconnaissance on the 29th on the east side of Mine Run. The assault on the 30th included the sharpshooters resulted in horrific losses including that of Casper Trepp (Egan, 1863). Trepp was leading the regiment against Rebel rifle pits when he was shot through the head. Roswell Weston commented that he felt there was no one suitable in the regiment to take his place (Hastings G. G., Letter to Lillie Devereaux , 1863). According to Regimental Chaplin Lorenzo Barber, they did manage to capture between 300 and 400 rebel prisoners (Murray, 2005). Hastings was hoping to be reassigned to the regiment, which had lost nearly 60 killed and wounded at Mine Run (Hastings G. G., Letter to Lillie Devereaux , 1863). Following Mine Run, the Union Army went into winter quarters at Brandy Station. Woodard Hodgson was sent to the US Hospital at Fairfax with an undisclosed injury in December but was back on the muster roll by the end of the month. Noah Olds however, deserted.

The end of 1863, also saw the numbers of Company H further reduced. At the start of 1863, there were 60 soldiers on paper belonging to the regiment, at the end, only 45. During the course of the year, eight deserted, one died, four were discharged, and two were transferred to the invalid corps. Winthrop and Hastings remained detailed out of the company[28]. Fisk, Schermerhorn, Olds, and Gardner were all recovering from wounds. Roswell Weston temporarily resigned his commission to recover from an attack of scurvy. Hastings visited Roswell in late November, and told Lillie

---

[28] Hastings had spent some time in New York and was so dissatisfied with the lack of patriotism and care for the soldiers, that he actually preferred being in Washington, a place he called "stupid" only a few months before (Hastings G. G., Letter to Lillie Devereaux, 1863).

Devereaux that Roswell seemed much better (Hastings G. G., Letter to Lillie Devereaux, 1863). On New Year's Eve, Akin Ingersoll would desert from the regiment as well. The actual strength of Company H was close to 36.

6 1864

While in some aspect the start of 1864 was quiet, in many ways it was not. Berdan was finally discharged from the regiment on January 2nd. Veterans that reenlisted were given a furlough of 35 days starting in February. Sylvester Loomis took the opportunity of the veteran furlough to desert. Noah Olds however returned to the Company. Company H was not involved in operations during the early months, however a major upheaval occurred that ended an era. With Casper Trepp dead, and Hiram Berdan relieved of command, the sharpshooters had started to decline in military appearance and drill. Charles Mattocks, formerly of the 17th Maine was moved over to command the sharpshooters in order to instill some order and refit the troops[29]. Mattocks in a letter home stated he wanted no part of the sharpshooters, and in fact had stated in a letter home on March 27th that he was "not less disgusted" by the

---

[29] At this time the sharpshooters had no staff grade officers in the field.

move. He knew they were lacking in military structure and discipline and hoped that after cleaning up the mess would be returned to the 17th. If Company H thought that life under Hastings and Trepp was difficult they had no idea how strict Mattocks could be. Unfortunately Company H would find out almost immediately after Mattocks dealt with Roswell Weston (Mattocks, 1994).

Weston had recently returned from his scurvy attack, serving as adjutant and very, very drunk. It was mentioned in Charles Mead's Diary that the sutlers obtained a stock of liquor on January 7th and it "caused some of the officers to feel quite happy." Mead gives special mention to Lt. Cotes of Company I, but his actions would be far superseded by Weston (Purdy, 2002). During dress parade, on April 14th, while still acting as adjutant, Roswell, according to Mattocks, was drunk and fell off of his horse. It took several men to remount him, and he was unable to get his feet back into the stirrups. Major Mattocks had Roswell arrested and brought before a courts martial. Mattocks didn't necessarily want to charge Weston with drunk and disorderly, stating that Weston was "of excellent family, well-educated and a most excellent adjutant." It just so happened that Mattocks hated drunks. In later letters, Mattocks is very happy to have removed Weston to set an example. Several officers, Michael McGeough among them wrote a letter to Mattocks asking that Weston be released. Mattocks asserted in his diary that the only use for that letter was the blank portion should he need additional stationary. In fact, Mattocks responded that a letter like this was "unmilitary" and unsolicited advice, in the future, would not "be taken notice of." Weston's courts martial started on April 24th where he attempted an affirmative defense where he stated that due to the need to take quinine for his various ailments, and due to the horse stumbling he fell out of the saddle. Weston had the support of several other officers, whom Mattocks termed his "drinking buddies" (Mattocks, 1994).

Roswell Weston resigned his commission for the last time and was dismissed from the army in May of 1864 (Foote, 2010). He would not be replaced in the ranks of company H, and it marks the last of the 7th militia's influence in the officer ranks of Company H. Additionally for the first time none of the top officers in the field were the upper class elite either, Michael McGeough was from Glens Falls and John Schermerhorn hailed from Schenectady. Neither had gone to Yale, or Harvard. Their family lineage did not include colonial founders or signers of association papers. McGeough was barely 20 years old. Far from being a lawyer, Schermerhorn was a machinist before the war.

The officer ranks were not the only place experiencing change. Clinton Loveridge, whose leg was amputated, was finally healthy enough to be transferred to the Invalid Corps in April. Edward Carmick of Ronkonkoma, who had been promoted to Sergeant before Chancellorsville was able to secure a promotion in the 124th New York, and left the Sharpshooters to become a Lieutenant. Martin V. Nichols and Marvin Hildebrandt were promoted to corporal.

Wilderness

On Wednesday, May 4th, company H entered the wilderness with roughly 30 men on the roster. Company H was led by Michael McGeough, the regiment was in the second brigade of the Third Division. The company formed as part of a skirmish line along with much of the regiment. A, C, and D were held in reserve. There wasn't much contact the first day; however by May 5th the regiment, enroute to Orange Court House and Brock Roads came in contact with rebel skirmishers. Here Mattocks was captured after trying to locate some of the sharpshooters (Mattocks, 1994). Mattocks would go through several internment camps most notably Oglethorpe. Additionally Martin V. Nichols, Orrin E. Doty and Barnard Gardner of Company H, along with about 10 other sharpshooters from the 1st regiment were captured on the 5th and sent down to Andersonville Prison (National Park Service, 1999). Almost instantly they were robbed of their belongings, mostly blankets and gum rubber ponchos. Orrin Doty managed to hide $10 in his hat. Orrin was able to buy two pounds of crackers with the money from a rebel sutler. While passing through the south a Rebel officer attempted to shoot Doty, however was stopped by the provost. This may indicate the reputation that sharpshooters had in the South (Doty O. E.).

The initial intent of the movement was to find out the strength and position of the enemy; however they ran into the Confederates who were waiting. The right of the line, held by Company A was devastated. They withdrew to Brock road, then to Orange road to rejoin the brigade (Stevens, 1892). The wilderness would further reduce the numbers of the regiment, and Company H was not exempt. Michael McGeough was wounded in the leg on the 7th and it required amputation, he ultimately would die from the wounds on the 22nd.

Spotsylvania

Leaving the Wilderness, the Sharpshooters moved towards Spotsylvania Court House on the 8th. Company H and the rest of the regiment moved towards Po River and came under fire from a battery that they had not seen. Moving off to a hill close by, they were exposed to firing on their flank. The next morning, they were sent to the front where they constructed fire pits with bayonets and tin plates. To make matters worse a heavy rain started to fall. Although casualties were light for the regiment, George Wiggins was wounded at Po River and Harvey Matthews at Harris House.

Cold Harbor

What was left of the 1st Regiment was fighting in Birney's Division in the second brigade under Colonel Tannatt. In late May, Grant kept his push to flank around Lee's army. Lee was able to dig in behind Totopotomoy Creek, and Grant ordered an attack on May 30th. Hancock's II Corps, was to cross the creek and attack the center of the Confederate line. Initially Birney was held on the heights overlooking swift run. It was jungle like, hot and infested with insects. Rations were short, and although there was not a general engagement for Birney's men, there were frequent, deadly skirmishes. Once across the creek they were under constant fire.

John Snyder was mortally wounded by a shot through the lungs in one of these skirmishes on the 31st. John had been attempting to recover at the hospital in Washington; however he ultimately passed in July of 1864. On June 1st, they were on the far right flank of the Union Army near Swift Run and they began to leave for Cold Harbor after dark. Birney was held in reserve to exploit a breakthrough, however, Hancock had not learned of a breakthrough fast enough to put Birney's men into service (Rhea, 2007). Aaron Fuller was wounded during the assaults on the third.

General Grant, in his memoirs stated "I have always regretted that the last assault at Cold Harbor was ever made. I might say the same thing of the assault of the 22d of May, 1863, at Vicksburg. At Cold Harbor no advantage whatever was gained to compensate for the heavy loss we sustained" (Grant, 1885). On June 12th Grant disengaged Lee's army and moved south toward Petersburg.

Siege of Petersburg

The Siege started with only 40 men on paper left in the company, however, the reality was that far fewer men were actually able to take the field. Hastings and Winthrop were reassigned. John Snyder lay mortally wounded in a hospital. Aaron Fuller and Harvey

Mathews were in a hospital recovering from wounds. Martin Nichols, Barnard Gardner and Orrin Doty were all languishing at Andersonville. John Brower, William Conklin, Akin Ingersoll and Edwin Lynde were all out sick. Hancock's II corps arrived at Petersburg on June 15. Repeated failures of assaults led to Meade ordering the II corps to attack on the right on the 18th. Birney was in the center of the Union attack and William Hicks would be killed as the Sharphooters fired in support of a charging Union Army at the former racetrack known as Newmarket. The attack had initial success but was stopped by Confederate forces, forcing Meade to change plans and have the army dig in. On the 17th of July Lewis Soule was captured, he was presumed a deserter initially, but was later returned to muster out.

Peter Louis originally from Company B, was discharged for disability in August from the hospital in New York City. Of the seven Company B transfers into Company H, the only remaining member was William Gillian. Joyce, Foster and Campbell all deserted. Loveridge, Barber and Louis were all wounded and eventually discharged. Gillian transferred from Company B with the rank of Sergeant, but as was reduced in ranks upon entering Company H. He was transferred back into company B in August.

September 1864

In September, the original enlistments expired, and Winthrop, Hastings, William Conklin, George Wiggins, Michael Curry, Thomas Andrews, George Whitney, Eliphalet Hill, James Thorn,

John Schermerhorn, Ezra Soper and John Acker were all mustered out of the company. That left 23 on paper still enlisted. Nichols, Gardner, Soule and Doty were still prisoners of war. Mathews and Fuller were in the hospital wounded. In order to manage the diminishing ranks everyone left was transferred into Company D. Woodard Hodgson was promoted to Second Lieutenant in September and then Captain just before the second round of musters. William Henry Burroughs and William Nichols were promoted to sergeant. Philip Service was sent to the hospital sick just after the initial muster out, and Andrew Westervelt was sent sick in October.

Second Round of Musters November 1864

For those that enlisted in late 1861, they were mustered out in November of 1864. The company lost William Nichols, George Livingston, Harvey Matthews, James Fisk, Woodard Hodgson, William Henry Burroughs, John Brower, Edward Lynd, Horace Smith, Akin Ingersoll and George Lattin. Of the ten men left that remained, four were prisoners of war, two were sick in the hospital, one was in the hospital wounded. From Company D, they were then transferred to Company K. Once Company K mustered out, they were transferred to Company C of the 2nd US Sharpshooters. From there the sharpshooters disbanded and those left were sent to the 124th in March of 1865.

7 1865

As of March the roster consisted of several prisoners of war: Barnard Gardner, Lewis Soule, Martin Nichols, and Orrin Doty. Both Soule and Gardner were not listed as prisoners on their muster roll abstract. Gardner was listed as being sick in Alexandria and Soule was listed as a deserter. The remainder of the muster roll consisted of: Henry Ecker, Aaron Fuller, Charles Hicks, Marvin Hillabrant, Sylvester Lawson, Philip Service, and Isaac Smith. Charles Hicks was sent to City Point Hospital, acting a guard. Aaron Fuller was acting as a teamster with Division Headquarters. Isaac Smith and Marvin Hillabrant were both promoted to corporal prior to moving to the 124th and kept that rank while there. Sylvester Lawson was promoted from sergeant to 2nd Lieutenant of Company H, 124th NY on March 14th. There would be only a brief reunion with former Sharpshooter Edward Carmick, he was killed April 1st in fighting near Boydton and Quaker Roads. In May, Andersonville was liberated, freeing Martin Nichols, Orrin Doty and Barnard Gardner.

On June 1st, the 124th mustered out of service. Charles Hicks and Isaac Smith, transferred to Company D of the 93rd New York for final muster on June 29th. The last remaining sharpshooter, Noah Olds was on the books until 1866 as he had to recoup the time lost during his absence without leave however he had been mustered out with the company in September of 1864.

For all the indications that Company H was different because of the relative wealth and societal standing of its officers or the deep connection with the 7th militia, their record is one of a few, elite regiments during the war. Not only were the officers and men on many occasions cited for bravery, many served in greater capacities after leaving Company H: In the Volunteer Army, George Hastings achieved the rank of brevet Colonel; Joseph Hall was a Lieutenant with the 1st Long Island Regiment; George Hall was a sergeant with the 14th New York Heavy Artillery; Clinton Loveridge served as a Lieutenant with the Invalid Corps, John Cooley became a Major (brevet Lt. Colonel) with the 148th. Other served in various regiments as privates. In the regular army: William Winthrop achieved the rank of Colonel with the Judge Advocates; Albert Barrett, Lieutenant with the Quartermaster Department; Frederick Peet, Lieutenant in the Marine Corps; Jacob Crawford, private in the 6th US Cavalry; Joseph Matthews and Orrin B. Smith went into the Navy; John Cooley after the war ended gained a commission as a Lieutenant in the 13th Regiment.

8 AFTER THE WAR

In total, 111 men called company H home during the course of the war. There are some soldiers for which, no pre or post war record exists. Whether they used false names or just lived their lives in obscurity, there is no clear way to identify who they were, or where they came from. In some cases no post war record exists for the simple fact that the solider did not survive the war. The losses in company H included Black, Rouse, Vincent and Newberry to disease; Phelps, Hicks, McGeough, Snyder, and Carmick to wounds. Many of the deserters also left no post war record including: Burtless, Edgerly, Mullen, Joyce, Sands, and Seaman.

Many members of the company returned to their lives before the war. Others took the opportunity to seek out life elsewhere. Fifty former soldiers lived in New York after the war, five lived in New Jersey, four ventured out to California, three moved to Illinois, three moved to Pennsylvania, two lived in Canada, two to Indiana, two to Michigan, two in Washington D.C. and two in Iowa. Members also moved to Texas, Wisconsin, Utah, Virginia, Oregon, Kansas, and Connecticut. Of the members who filled out a census after the war; 75 were married, and 63 reported having children. Employment after the war was as varied as the locations. Fourteen were farmers, eight were carpenters, four clerks, three were involved in politics, three were doctors of some sort, other jobs included: policemen, railroad employees, civil service, dentist, harness maker, wagon maker, insurance agent, pattern maker, shoemaker, pack train guide, restaurant owner, lumber dealer, and grain merchant. Harvey Doolittle could not work as a result of his wounds.

Sixty-three members applied for pensions, 60 of which were granted; Larrason and Whitney died before the pensions could be issued. Foster was listed as a deserter, and therefore not eligible for a pension. Forty-three widows applied for pensions, as did the mothers of Edward Carmick, John Snyder and David Phelps. Nathan Rouse's father applied for his pension. Of those pension requests, 40 were granted. During the course of their lives nine former company H soldiers would check into a soldier's home, five of which were in the Bath Soldier's home.

Of the 83 men that have definitive dates of the death, the average age of death for a member of company H was 64 years old. The youngest to pass was David Phelps at age 19, the oldest George P. Walters who was 96. Walters, however was not the last surviving member of Company H. That honor went to Sylvester Lawson who passed in 1931. Of the surviving members of Company H, 53 lived to see the US fight in another war, this time with Spain. Nineteen saw the US enter World War I, 17 would live to see its conclusion.

The Company was indeed elite, and despite the personal feelings of Berdan and Mattocks, their records for bravery stands as testament to their dedication to the causes of liberty. Whatever the personal motivations of the individual members may have been, they proved in blood, on numerous battlefields that they are worthy of the designation of elite.

LONG ISLAND COMPANY

Major George Hastings

Captain William Winthrop

(Pictured as Lt. Colonel, JAG)

LONG ISLAND COMPANY

2nd Lieutenant Frederick T. Peet

2nd Lieutenant Michael McGeough

1st Sergeant John T. Schermerhorn

Sergeant Orrin Doty

Sergeant Barnard Gardner

Cpl. George F. Hall

(Pictured as Sgt. 14th Heavy Artillery)

Pvt. Edward Carmick

(Pictured with 124th NY)

Pvt. Richard Lansing Boyd

Pvt. Sylvester Lawson

(Pictured as Lieutenant, 124th NY)

Harry D. Tyler

9 BIOGRAPHICAL SKETCHES

Captains

George G. Hastings

George Granberry (often Cranberry) Hastings was from a historic and wealthy family tree, the Granberry/Hastings line hailed from the Norfolk County area of Virginia. The Granberrys were plantation owners, and likewise slaveholders (50 Dollars Reward, 1820)[30]. They accounted for five Revolutionary War veterans, with Moses and George Granberry being from Norfolk (Ancestor Search, 2013).

Following a move north, and now residing at their 32 Pierpont Street address in Brooklyn, the Hastings family was no stranger to comfort. In 1850, the household was valued at $110,000 and identified two servants from England and one from Ireland. Census data from 1860 reflects the 1853 passing of George Sr (Legal Notices, 1853), and the untimely death of George G.'s wife Laura Helen Curtis in 1859, shortly after giving birth to their daughter Edith.

George stood 5'10" had blue eyes and brown hair. He had moved to

---

[30] There are at least 3 surviving runaway slave ad's posted by Granberry relatives in the North Carolina General Advertiser/ Edenton Gazette, including two by James Granberry (1807,1809)and one by Thomas Granberry (1820)

Essex, New Jersey along with his mother, Mary Louisa Granberry, her sister Caroline Granberry, and his brother Eastburn[31] and had increased the number of Irish-born servants to four (US Census Bureau, 1850). The value of the property was at $50,000 and Mary's personal estate at $10,000 probably reflecting the settlement of debts from George's death.

Like many families of privilege, education and community-minded activities were important. The Hastings were no different, George Sr., a wealthy merchant, was a trustee of the Brooklyn City Hospital, Eastburn had studied to become an architect, George attended Yale, studied commercial law in New York City and spent a year in Harvard (Powtin, 1894). George graduated in 1854 and was a member of Yale's Alpha Delta Phi Society (Alpha Delta Phi, 1870). After graduation he served as a vice president of the Mercantile Library Association (Establishment of a Mercantile Library Association, 1857) as well as a director of the Brooklyn Philharmonic Society (Stiles H. R., 1870).

George practiced law in New York from the time he graduated Yale until the start of the war. Like his father, George sat on the board of directors for a fire insurance company (Mechanics' Fire Insurance Company, 1859). The offices were located on Montague Street, which would later become the recruiting office for the Sharpshooters.

George was married to Laura Helen Curtis prior to the war, and had a daughter, Edith. Laura unfortunately passed in 1859. Prior to the war Hastings was friends with John Wilson, Lieutenant of Company B. Eventually Wilson would be promoted to Major (Stevens, 1892). George had met his fellow sharpshooter officer William Winthrop while at Yale. Through William, George most likely met Lillie Devereux, a woman that he would fall in love with after the passing of Laura, only to be spurned during the closing months of the war. Lillie had quite the history, having been directly responsible for WHL Barnes, a student at Yale, being dismissed for having impugned the dignity of Lillie (Farrell, 2002). She too had been married and her spouse passed in 1859 as well. Their letters

---

[31] Jane Clemens and Patrick Freel (identified as a coachman)

indicate that they spent many happy days prior to the start of the war, and George fully expected to marry Lille, and was shocked instead when she promised herself to Grinfill Blake.

Winthrop's friendship with Hastings will be the foundation for a strong officer corps, providing the leadership for the company. Winthrop and Peet acted as the balance to Hastings firm, tough brand of leadership. Major Hastings never fully recovered from the wounds sustained in the saddle, and the War Department would not let him back into the field. As the war closed he would be brevetted the rank of Colonel. Once back in civilian life he moved to Ossining, and did return to the profession of law, but soon after took a civil service position as a customs inspector with the New York port of entry. In 1871 he was stricken with paralysis that may have been related to his war injury (Powtin, 1894). He died October 20, 1873 and was buried in Greenwood Cemetery. Edith Hastings later unsuccessfully sued along with her aunts in Superior Court to get title to an inheritance from their mother's (Edith's grandmother) property (Jones, 1891). George's father and mother have marked graves at Greenwood, however, George, Eastburn (1884), Adelaide (1882), his daughter Edith (1934) and his wife Laura are buried at the plot without markers.

William Woolsey Winthrop

William Winthrop was born August 3rd, 1831 in New Haven, Connecticut to Francis Bayard Winthrop and Elizabeth Woolsey. Francis' father, Also Francis Bayard Winthrop, had inherited part of Block Island, in the Long Island Sound which had been in the Winthrop Family, since John Winthrop, former governor of Connecticut. Francis had passed by 1850, and Elizabeth maintained the household, worth roughly $12,000, with William, his four siblings and the family's three servants (US Census Bureau, 1850). They were descendent of the famous Winthrop's of Boston, his ancestor John having helped found the colony in Massachusetts.

William followed his brother Theodore to Yale, where his uncle Reverend Theodore Dwight Woolsey was the president. While at Yale, he met

Theodore Weston, who also held an interest in racing and had organized Yale and Harvard's first regatta, of which Winthrop participated. Weston would eventually marry William's sister Sarah. William was awarded the Berkeley Scholarship in 1851 and a scholarship for English composition. He, Robert Peet (brother of fellow sharpshooter Frederick Peet), Weston (brother of fellow sharpshooter Roswell Weston), and George Tuckmann (later of Company D) were underclassmen together (Catalogue of the Officers and Students in Yale College 1850-1851., 1850). After graduating from Yale, he proceeded to Harvard for further training in law. Upon finishing his degree he opened a law practice in Boston, followed by several years as a frontier lawyer in Minnesota (Kastenberg, 2009).

By 1860 the 5'6", grey-eyed, brown-haired Winthrop had returned to New York and was living with his sister Laura and her family in Staten Island (US Census Bureau, 1860). He opened a law firm Winthrop and Little, with his college friend, Robbins Little (Powtin, 1894).

While living in Staten Island he became friendly with other New England transplants, notably the Shaw family, fellow ardent abolitionists whose soon-to-be famous son, Robert Gould Shaw would serve in the 7th NY Militia with William and his brother Theodore. Robert and William would land up in Company F, and Theodore in Company I (Swinton, 1870). Robert, whose letters were well preserved, wrote to his mother during the war to report that the Winthrop's were faring well (Shaw, 1999). It would be no surprise that the Winthrop brothers and Robert would view the war in a vastly different light then most others in 1861[32]. While not totally uncommon, joining the war to end slavery was not the standard motivation in 1861, in fact there were points early in the war where Lincoln feared the reaction to fighting a war whose aim was slavery rather than keeping together a shattered country[33].

---

[32] Winthrop would suggest in a letter to Frederick Peet in 1863 that General Beauregard once he surrenders, should be forced to turn his sword over to a "Colored Corporal" and then be marched off guarded by "colored soldiers" (Peet F. T., Civil War Letters and Documents of Frederick Tomlinson Peet, 1917)
[33] James Macpherson ties together several episodes where Lincoln expressly overturned emancipation, probably the most famous being Major General

While neither brother would eclipse the lasting fame that Robert Gould Shaw would attain, William would one day rise to a prominence of his own as a military Judge Advocate General, writing books that are still in use today[34]. Theodore had gained fame as an author, however many of Theodore's works were published posthumously by his sister. Reminiscent of the untimely death of poet Joyce Kilmer in WWI, Theodore's writing career was cut short as he was the first high-ranking officer killed in action during the Civil War. Before the battle of Bull Run, the 7th had been dismissed from federal service at this point and William had returned home. Theodore however was able to secure a promotion to major, and was attached to General Butler's staff. He volunteered to assist General Ebenezer Pierce in launching an attack from Fortress Monroe up the Peninsula with the idea that they could take Richmond eventually. As they marched towards Big Bethel, they ran into a strongly entrenched Confederate force. Winthrop leapt up on a fallen tree to urge his men forward when he was shot through the heart.

William, along with brother-in-law, Theodore Weston, went to retrieve the body, and return it to New Haven for the funeral. After the ceremony, William returned to New York in search of a regiment to join, and enlisted with his friend, and fellow alumni George Hastings. At the time of enlistment, William stood 5'6" with grey eyes and brown hair. After the war, William transferred to the regular Army after the war ended as a Major in the Judge Advocate General. In 1877, he married Alice Worthington, who was the grand-daughter of Governor Thomas Worthington, a founder of Ohio. Alice was born in July of 1851 at Liberty, Virginia, and shortly after being married, fell gravely ill, and William had to request a temporary delay in his assignment while he tended to her.

His job took him and his wife around the United States; he lived in Washington D.C., San Francisco and Minnesota before settling finally in New Jersey. As a JAG he wrote one of the foremost books on military law, Military Law and Precedents. Winthrop is still cited in military case

---

Fremont's freeing of slaves in Missouri, and Lincoln's overturning of the order.
[34] Military Law 1886 and Military Law and Precedents 1896

appeals today, and has been cited by the Supreme Court on occasion. He served as a professor of Law at West Point from 1886 to 1890 (Powtin, 1894). He retired from military service in July of 1895. In 1896 Winthrop was awarded an honorary Doctor of Laws from Georgetown University.

In addition to his legal pursuits, Winthrop also became interested in Colonial Massachusetts history, donating a series of papers from John Winthrop to the Colonial Society of Massachusetts in 1880 and was elected a corresponding member in 1899 (Young 1899).

He passed on April 8, 1899 from a sudden heart attack, and there is no known record of his burial. Alice applied for, and received a pension in 1899 and remained in New Jersey until her death in 1900.

Lieutenants

Frederick Tomlinson Peet Jr.

Frederick was born July 8th 1841 in Brooklyn, New York to Frederick Peet Sr. and Elizabeth Roe. The Peet's first landed in America in April of 1635 when John Peet arrived in Stratford, Connecticut. William Peet, helped to defend Brooklyn with Colonel Ward during the Revolution. William was wounded and taken prisoner in April of 1777 (Peet F. T., 1896). Fred Sr., an importer of silk whose property was valued at $15,000 and whose personal estate was $20,000 was also a superintendent of a Sabbath school, formed a temperance society in June of 1829, and was a member of the First Presbyterian Church (Stiles H., 1867).

Frederick Jr. lived with his family and four servants on Peirrepont Street, not far from the Hastings[35]. Peet attended Brooklyn Polytechnic and Churchill Military Academy (Sing Sing) prior to the war. He like many other jumped at the chance to join the 7th New York Militia, and was enrolled in company H (Swinton, 1870). He preferred a post in the regular army and through various connections with his father attempted to gain a commission. While waiting for a regular army post he had accepted a commission as a lieutenant in another regiment. Fortunately for Hastings and Winthrop, that infantry regiment converted to artillery and Peet ultimately declined the offer (Peet F. T., Personal Experiences in the Civil War, 1905).

Hastings was walking on the bridge to Montague Street when he coincidentally ran into Frederick and offered him a commission. Aside from living close together, George had studied law as a clerk under Frederick's brother William, and William had acted as referee in lawsuits that the Hastings brothers filed against Edgar J Bartow.

---

[35] According to Peet, Hastings lived on the corner of Pierrepont and Hicks, while the Peets were on Pierrepont and Clark.

After recovering from his wounds, Peet was able to accept his commission with the Marine Corps. He participated in the assault on Battery Wagner, and was present, although did not participate in the assault on Fort Sumter. Peet remained with the Marines after the war and was promoted to the rank of 1st lieutenant. In the years after the war, he would purchase a ranch in Los Angeles, however Frederick would return home to Brooklyn to act as General Manager of the I&W Railway Company. He joined post 37 of the GAR and listed himself as a coal merchant. He married Cornilia Starwell in 1887, though tragically she passed in 1889. At the urging of his children, Peet would publish his letters and then a diary of his wartime experiences, before he passed on January 29, 1925. He was buried in Greenwood Cemetery.

Roswell Weston Jr.

Roswell Weston was born in May of 1839 to Frederick and Elizabeth Weston, a family of farmers from Sandy Hill, Washington County, New York. The Weston family was involved in early New York politics, with Roswell's namesake serving on the 39th New York legislature from Washington County. The property was worth roughly $10,000 in 1850, and they had two Irish laborers to help maintain the farm (US Census Bureau, 1850). In 1855 Roswell attended Harvard and was a member of the Natural History Society ((Harvard University, 1855). He may have also attended one semester at Yale in 1859 (Yale University, 1859). By 1860, Roswell was living in Agnes Livingston's boarding house in Brooklyn and was working as a clerk (US Census Bureau, 1860).

His brother, Theodore, attended Yale in 1849, meeting William Winthrop and becoming involved with the regatta. Theodore married William's sister Chauncy in 1861 and had a child also named Theodore (Dwight, 1874). Theodore traveled down to Big Bethel to help William retrieve his brother's body.

Roswell joined the 7th Militia once the call went up for volunteers, and served with his brother-in-law William in Company F (Swinton, 1870). Following the dismissal of the 7th, Roswell would once again follow

William into further service with the Sharpshooters. He would not, however, enlist right away.

It was not until December 11th, 1861 that he joined the regiment in Washington D.C. Weston was sent to Howe's brigade to serve in the Quartermaster Department from April 8th – July 9th of 1862. He rose to the rank of 2nd Lieutenant after Peet resigned to accept his commission in the Marines. He was promoted to 1st Lieutenant September of 1862. He served as the Regimental Adjutant starting in February of 1863.

His attack of scurvy in October of 1863 left him so disfigured; his own friends could not recognize him. He was dismissed, reinstated, deserted, returned but was found to be drunk on duty faced a courts martial and was cashiered out of the army. He lived at 210 S. 41st St in Pennsylvania after the war; he married Elizabeth Wilcox in April of 1865.

Roswell was later a manager at the Schuylkill Navigation Company, and was living in Wernersville, Pennsylvania when he passed October 18, 1903. He was buried three days later in Sandy Hill, New York, most likely at the family plot in Union Cemetery. Elizabeth attempted to file a widow's pension in 1908 but due to Weston's discharge was not eligible.

Michael McGeough

Lt. McGeough was born in Sandy Hills, New York in 1834. He was 27 when he enlisted in Company H as a corporal on August 18, 1861. He was promoted seven days later to sergeant, and almost a year to the day later, Lieutenant. He was in command of the company during the months that Roswell Weston was away from duty, predominately October 1863, December through February of 1864, and April of 1864. He was severely wounded at the Battle of the Wilderness, and died on May 22nd as a result of infections from the wound. He was buried in Washington D.C. but his body was exhumed in May 27, 1864 by John McGeough. There is a monument in downtown Glens Falls inscribed with his name.

Woodard Hodgson

Hodgson was 20 when he enlisted as a private from his hometown of Black Brook, NY on August 11, 1861. There are several Hodgson's listed in the history of Black Brook including: John/Jonathan who was a founder of Black Brook in the 1840, and served as a supervisor and town clerk, and four children who were baptized at the Episcopal Church: Joseph, Eliza, William and Mary Ann (Hurd, 1880). While in the Sharpshooters he was listed as either Woodard or Woodward, and on the 1870 census, but afterward he is listed as John.

He would attain the rank of corporal in November of 1861, Sergeant in April of 1862 and 2nd Lieutenant in September of 1864. Following his transfer to Company D, he would be promoted to Captain taking over for Oliver J Hetherington. He would be mustered out in November of 1864. During the war he was wounded three times, in the head at Charles City Crossroads, in the face at Chancellorsville and lastly in the head at Mine Run. He moved to Odgen, Utah after the war where he was junior vice commander of the James B McKean GAR Post. He was an engineer and railroad constructor. He passed November 7th, 1903 and was buried in the Ogden City Cemetery.

1st Sergeants

Albert Reed Barrett

Albert was born in New York City, to Benjamin Barrett and Elizabeth Allen on July 14, 1841. Benjamin had attended Bowdoin College, graduating in 1832. He then studied at Cambridge in 1834 and Harvard in 1838. In addition to serving as a preacher in a Unitarian Church, Benjamin also was involved in a roofing business. He wrote a number of books[36], and was head of the Swedenborgian Church (Class of 1832, 1895). In many ways Albert would be different from Hastings, Winthrop, Peet and Weston, but the similarities of coming from a well-connected well-to-do family cannot be ignored.

Much like the Winthrop's, Barrett descended from early settlers of Massachusetts. His ancestor Thomas settled in Braintree in 1635. He was directly descended from Oliver Barrett, who served as a minuteman in the battle of Lexington, and who was later killed at the second battle of Stillwater. Albert attended military school in Yonkers, New York and then Eastman's Business College in Poughkeepsie (Barrett W. , 1888). As soon as the call went up for volunteers Albert joined the 7th and was assigned to Company I along with Theodore Winthrop (Swinton, 1870).

Albert had enlisted as a second sergeant with the sharpshooters on September 25, 1861. He was promoted to 1st Sergeant in October of 1861 and to 2nd Lieutenant in October of 1862 along with his transfer to Company D. He was discharged with a brevetted rank of 1st Lieutenant in the fall of 1862 due to disability. He would re-enlist as a Lieutenant with the Quartermaster Department near Nashville, Tennessee where he would start his post war career in banking (Barrett W., 1888).

---

[36] His works include: New Dispensation, Letters to Beecher on the Divine Trinity, Letters to Beecher on Future Life, Swedenborg and Channing, Golden City, New View of Hell, Heaven Revealed, Question Answered, Footprints on the New Age, and True Catholicism (Barrett W. , 1888).

Albert married Marie Louise Barnes in September of 1865, and would move to Virginia by 1880 ultimately settling in Germantown, Pennsylvania. They had three children, Charles, William and May. Mary unfortunately passed in 1881 at the age of 38. Following the war, Albert was banker and studied medicine in the evenings at the University of Nashville where he would graduate in 1877 (Stedman, 1910). Even though he was a doctor, Albert did not stop working as a banker, and worked as a bank examiner for the Government, and published a book Modern Methods of Banking and Practical Book Keeping, this is still in publication today. In the preface Albert noted he worked as a banker, bank examiner and accountant (Barrett A. R., 1907). Though his death certificate lists him as an expert accountant that was only in the later years of his life (Pennsylvania, Philadelphia City Death Certificates, 1803–1915, 2010). Albert died in January of 1910 as a result of complications from an operation on his stomach (Medical Society of the State of Pennsylvania, 1910). He is buried at the Greenwood Cemetery in Brooklyn; however he does not have a gravestone.

John T. Schermerhorn

John was a 25 year old, 5'11" machinist from Schenectady, New York when he enlisted as a corporal in Brooklyn on August 19, 1861. Born April 26, 1836 to Bartholomew Teller and Adaline Schermerhorn, John was descendent of Revolutionary War Veteran also named Bartholomew, the Schermerhorn family was native to a province in North Holland, with the first Schermerhorn landing in American before 1648 (Laer, 1908). Bartholomew was a farmer whose property was valued near $5,000 (US Census Bureau, 1860).

John had blue eyes and brown hair and was recruited by George Hastings. He was promoted to sergeant in July of 1862 and 1st Sergeant in April of 1863. Schermerhorn was severely wounded at Gettysburg, yet refused a discharge. He was mustered out of the company as commander in September of 1864 and was so beloved by his comrades that they presented him with a sword that remains on display today. The sword was engraved with: Presented to 1st Sgt. John T. Schermerhorn 1st REG'T USSS by the Men of Co H, NYV. Additionally his forage cap and first sergeant chevrons remain some of the last surviving examples of Berdan uniforms and are available to view at the Milwaukee County Historical Society. Schermerhorn had sewn the III corps red diamond into his sergeant strips, as opposed to the standard green diamond.

Post War he moved to Milwaukee, WI with his wife Georgiana and worked in several engineering related jobs before becoming a toy maker. He passed in December, 1916 and is buried in the Forest Home Cemetery in Milwaukee.

John Jay Slifer

John was born October 20, 1832 in New York, and by the age of 16 was working as a silversmith (US Census Bureau, 1860).

He enlisted in Company H as a 5'7" dark haired, dark eyed, corporal on September 16, 1861. He was promoted to Sergeant in July of 1862, and 1st Sergeant in April of 1862, He deserted the company in April of 1863 from the hospital where he was mending from wounds to the shoulder and hip.

Post war he would own a restaurant in Philadelphia, where he lived at 913 Franklin Street, with his wife Sarah Goetchieus, son Frank, and daughter Jane (US Census Bureau, 1880). He died October 18, 1893 from sclerosis of the liver, and is buried in the North Laurel Hill Cemetery (Philadelphia City Archives, 2010). Frank was working as a Doctor at the time of John's death.

Sergeants

Edward Carmick

Sgt. Carmick was 20, stood 5'9" with blue eyes and light hair and was a farmer when he was recruited from Lakeland, New York on October 7, 1861. He was born in Philadelphia, Pennsylvania, the son of Evelina and Stephen Carmick. While in California in the late 1850's, Stephen contracted a fever that left him unable to do physical labor. Enlisting as a private, he was promoted to Sgt. April of 1863. In April of 1864, he would transfer, as a Sgt to the 124th New York, Company F. He was promoted to Lieutenant 18 days later and Captain in August of 1864. Wounded at Spotsylvania in May of 64, and at the Plank Road in October of 64, he returned both times only to be killed on April 1, 1865 as he was leading a charge near Petersburg.

Truly respected and loved by his men, they carefully buried their captain and marked the tree at the corner of Boydton and Quaker roads. His mother Evelina left from Lakeland to retrieve the body. General Gibbon detailed two teams and men to disinter Edward and he furnished a metal coffin. In 1866 Evelina, Edward's mother, sent a letter to Colonel Wegyant thanking him for taking care in burying and marking the body (Weygant, 1877).

He was reinterred at the Lake Ronkonkoma Cemetery with a large monument marking his burial plot. Evelina applied for a pension on September 8, 1865 and received a pension of $20 a month until her death in October of 1903 (National Archives and Records Administration, 2008).

Harvey Doolittle

Harvey was born in 1827 to Adrastus Doolittle and Hannah Higby. In 1850 Adrastus and Hannah were living in Manhattan, along with their children; Harvey, Mary, Adrastus and Emeline. Living with them also was Ann McElroy, an Irish servant. Harvey was 5'10" with brown eyes and black hair, working as a druggist (US Census Bureau, 1850). His father was a doctor who was born in Vermont, and was well known for helping cancer sufferers (Local News, 1895).

By 1860, Harvey was living with the Bostwicks in Babylon and working as a painter (US Census Bureau, 1860). He was promoted to corporal in October of 1861 and Sergeant 20 days later. He was discharged in 1862. He then enlisted in the local regiment of volunteers, the 127th NY company I as a Sgt. In 1863 he was returned to the rank of private (New York, Town Clerks' Registers of Men Who Served in the Civil War, ca 1861-1865). He was wounded and discharged for disability again in May of 1865.

His wounds never allowed him to work after the war, though he listed himself as a painter. Harvey was often found at church and Sunday school. According to the 1870 census, his wife was Antoinette Wood, and two children Albert and Emily were living in Brooklyn. He moved in with his widowed sister at 97 Bergen Street in Brooklyn. Harvey died of a heart attack in December of 1895 just prior to the start of a church service. He is laid to rest in the Evergreen cemetery in Brooklyn, NY (Local News, 1895). He was a member of GAR post 77.

Orrin Erastus Doty

Orrin was 18, and stood 5'8" when he was signed on in Spencertown on November 5, 1861. He was a descendent of Edward Doty, a Mayflower emigrant (Doty E. A., 1897). His parents were Orange and Catherine Doty; Orange being a stone mason, had served in the War of 1812 (Records of the Department of Veterans Affairs). The value of Orange's property was $400 (US Census Bureau, 1870). His Grandfather, William Doty may have served as a minuteman in the revolution, and may have even joined in the War of 1812 (Doty E. A., 1897).

Orrin was captured at the wilderness on May 5th 1864. He was taken to Andersonville Prison in Georgia. Doty managed to survive the horrific conditions of Andersonville, and later Florence. Upon rescue he was given a meal of ham, bread and coffee. He lamented the meal, reasoning that so many died after the meal due to overeating after being starved for many months. Orrin had entered the army at 165 pounds and left Florence at only 96 (Doty O. E.).

Post war, Orrin became a Wagon maker living at 90 Main St. in Newark, NJ. He married Anna and fathered four children: Wilber, Ida, May and Glen. Doty later wrote his memories down, he was critical of leadership, however, this did not stop him from attending a Prisoner of War dinner held in 1886 by Dr. G. W. Bassett at the Newark Hotel (A Reception at the Newark Hotel, 1886). In 1899, he joined GAR post 99. Despite all of his ailments, many related to his time in Andersonville, Orrin lived until August 31st, 1920. He is buried in Newark Cemetery. The Doty and Fisk families are related through Nathaniel Fisk (Pierce, 1896), who married the daughter of Mercy Doty (Doty E. A., 1897). On some paperwork Orrin refers to himself as Erastus.

Barnard Cornelius Gardner

Barnard, a 5'7" carpenter, was living in Huntington in 1860 with his parents Henry and Angeline Bort, and five siblings (US Census Bureau, 1860). He had been born in Lenox, in 1841. His grandfather, Jacob Gardinier was a Captain in the Tryon County militia and had been wounded at the battle of Oriskany in 1777. The earliest arriving Gardner was Jacob Janse Gardenier who arrived from the Netherlands between 1620 and 1638, marrying into the Kinderhook family.

Barnard went to Babylon to pass his qualifications for the sharpshooters and enlisted on August 24, 1861. He was promoted to corporal October 31st, 1861 and sergeant July 15th, 1862. He was wounded at Gettysburg, discharged in September of 1864.

After the war he married Harriet A. Louis and had four children: Elizabeth, Cornelius, Julia and Marie. He continued in the carpenter trade, unfortunately falling off a ladder to his death in June of 1910. He is buried in Addison Rural Cemetery. Barnard has a living relative.

Eliphalet C. Hill

Eliphalet was born in July of 1837 to William and Mary Hill in Islip, New York. William, a caulker, had eight children. Eliphalet stood 5'8" with grey eyes and brown hair and was working as a carpenter when he enlisted as a private in Company H on September 24, 1861. He was promoted to Corporal July 15th 1862 and Sergeant October 31st, 1863. He was sent sick to the US General Hospital in October of 1862. He was mustered out of the company in September 16th 1864.

Eliphalet was elected junior vice commander of GAR post 538, William Gurney. After the war he returned to Bay Shore and lived with his parents and sister, while working as a boatman. Not much is written of Hill aside from minor notes in the paper (He was called to jury duty in 1898, he was a trustee of the Bay Shore fire patrol). By 1900 he was living with his sister Melvina and her husband Edward Dickenson (US Census Bureau, 1900). He lived in Bayshore until his death July 3rd, 1920.

Henry Clay Niles

Henry was born to Milton and Christina Niles in Spencertown, New York in 1836. Milton may have worked as the town's postmaster (Skinner, 1830). He was given the rank of Sergeant on October 29 1861, but was discharged due to disability March 26th 1862. Henry was 5'6" with blue eyes and flaxen hair, was responsible for recruiting six soldiers in the Austerlitz area. Orrin Doty was under the impression that Henry was to lead his own company (Doty O. E.). Betsy Phelps referred to him as recruiting her son David in her pension papers (National Archives and Records Administration, 2008). In addition to Phelps and Doty, Henry recruited: George Vincent, William Nichols, Edwin Pulver, and Melanthenon Sanders.

In 1870 he was living in Washington D.C. with his wife Rosa, brother Ulysses and several servants. He was working as a clerk (US Census Bureau, 1870). Rosa applied for a pension in 1890 and was listed as a widow by 1878 in the Washington City Directories.

Henry C. Smith Jr.

Smith was a 25 year old, 5'10" clerk from Babylon when the war started; he entered the service on August 26, 1861. Henry was quickly promoted to corporal in October of 1861 and sergeant 18 days later. He was discharged in September of 1862 by order of General Dix for disability. He remained in the Suffolk County Militia (16th NYSM). Henry was captain of Company B, and assisted in quelling the riots in Jamaica, Queens where protesters had attempted to burn warehouses of military goods.

Henry was married to Sarah and worked as a farmer and general painter. He passed on February 9th 1920 and is buried in the Babylon Rural Cemetery. Henry applied for a pension in 1872, and Sarah applied for a widow's pension in 1925.

Horace Smith

Horace Smith, was born to Charles and Betsy Smith in 1839. Charles had emigrated from Canada originally. By 1850 the family had moved to Willsboro in Essex, New York. In 1860, Charles, Horace and his brother Wilber were all working as masons. The Smith family was rather large; Horace had seven siblings (US Census Bureau, 1860). Horace stood 5'10" and had blue eyes. He enlisted on November 13, 1861 and was promoted to Corporal in July of 1862 and Sergeant in April of 1863. Horace was sent sick from Gaines Mills to the General Hospital at former President George Washington's Whitehouse Estate in Virginia in 1862. He was transferred to Company D with the company in September 1864 and was discharged October 7th 1864.

After the war he married Susan and worked as a laborer and mason. They were living in Westport in 1880, Horace was working as a laborer (US Census Bureau, 1880). He applied for a pension in 1880 and his wife applied for a widow's pension in 1883. Horace passed October 19th, 1880 and is buried in the Memorial Cemetery in Willsboro.

Corporals

John Deverson Acker

John Acker, sometimes written as Ackers, was born November 15, 1842 and was living in Oyster Bay working as a printer when he enlisted as a private in the sharpshooters on August 26, 1861. According to a passport application filed later in life, Acker, was 5'8" and had blue eyes. He was promoted to Corporal April of 1863 and was mustered out of the company in September of 1864.

After the war he was a postmaster in Roslyn and became the town clerk of Hempstead. He wrote the records for Hempstead in 1874. He was also a renowned 33rd degree Mason. In 1880 he lived in Roslyn with his wife Mary where he worked as a retail grocer (US Census Bureau, 1880). He joined GAR post 135 in 1888. In his later years he moved to Brooklyn, on 69 Warren Street where he was second deputy clerk and where he died of an apoplexy April 27th 1911. He is buried in the Hollis cemetery.

Jacob Crawford

Jacob's real name is Samuel B. Bruce. He was a 26 year old, 5'10", blue-eyed, brown-haired laborer when he enlisted in the army as a corporal on October 1, 1861. He was discharge in December of 1862 with a disability from a hospital in Washington D.C. He enlisted September 18th 1865 in the 6th US Cavalry and was assigned to Company M. On the muster sheet he listed himself as 25, and hailing from Durham, Connecticut. His height was also listed as 5'7". He was discharged September 1868 as a sergeant.

Bruce moved to San Antonio, Texas, where it is possible he was living with his wife Marcela Bruce and a son Cantuno Bruce. He however, was living alone by 1900, and he worked as a watchman and a fireman, stationary engineer until February 5th, 1916. He is buried in the San Antonio National Cemetery. In the national database for gravesites, Samuel is listed as Jacob Crawford.

George Allen Defendorf

George Defendorf, sometimes written as Defendorg on Army documents, was one of the two youngest soldiers to enlist in company H; he was just 16 years old. His father George was born in New York, but his mother Catherine was born in England. George Sr. was working as a lawyer in New York. They were considered well-to-do and employed Ann Sudlow as a servant (US Census Bureau, 1860). He was sent to New York City in early 1862 to recover from a disability, but never returned, however he was on the July 15th muster roll.

He was discharged for disability on September 17th, 1862. He returned to New York to live with his mother, wife Elizabeth, son Allen, and daughter Winifred. George worked there as a dentist (US Census Bureau, 1870). They lived at 273 East 77th St.

However the manner in which he married his wife was the cause of some local scandal. According to a series of 1893 New York Times articles, George had an affair with his future wife, Eliza Vandervoort, which resulted in a child and was forced to marry her at gunpoint on July 7th, 1865.

George passed April 7th, 1890 and is buried in Greenwood Cemetery, Eliza died shortly thereafter on July 7th 1891. At this point Louie Vandervoort claimed he was the illegitimate son of George and Eliza, and should receive a ninth interest in the Defendorf estate (valued at $125,000 per share). Yet Louie did not change his name until after the deaths of George and Eliza. Unfortunately for Winifred and Allen, they were forced to listen to the retelling of George, upon learning of Eliza's pregnancy ran off to the army. Upon his return, he was forced to marry her. However as the case wound down, it was discovered that the child of George and Eliza was in fact stillborn. Louie was in reality an illegitimate son of Eliza's sister Emma Vandervoort. The marriage, between George and Eliza was actually a fraud perpetrated by the Vandervoorts. Louie withdrew his complaint and was forced to pay $600 in damages to Allen and Winifred and along with the witnesses faced possible arrest for perjury.

James Henry Fisk

James was born to William and Abigail in 1841. The family which had lived in Stillwater, NY had moved by 1860 to Jay, NY. James lived there with his father, mother and sister Alzina who was at the time a school teacher. William was a retired farmer, whose property was valued at $500 (US Census Bureau, 1860). He died in April of 1861.

They were descendants of early settlers of Massachusetts. Captain Phinehas Fiske emigrated and then helped settle Wenham, becoming a freeman in 1642 and acting as the town's constable. His son John also served as constable for Wenham as well as selectman, and was wounded during King Philips War. His great-grandfather Nathaniel Fiske was a Quaker Preacher, who as a result of refusing to fight during the revolution, had his land confiscated (Pierce, 1896). James was 21 when he enlisted on October 26, 1861. He was promoted to Corporal in April of 1863. Fisk had been wounded at Locust Grove and spent all of December 1862 in the US General Hospital at Washington D.C. In late December he was transferred to the Hospital at Fairfax, VA. On his Company H muster roll abstract he is listed as Fisker or Fiske. He transferred, along with the company to Company D.

James applied for a pension directly at the war's end, and married Mary, his first wife, in December of that year. Mary passed in 1868 and he married Margaret Simpson, in 1872, they had six children together. In 1900 they were living in Jay, where James was working as a carpenter (US Census Bureau, 1900). James died in September of 1917 in Hudson Falls, New York.

George F. Hall

George was born September 3, 1837 in Madison, New York. He was living with his father George, a clergyman, and mother Almira in Smithfield, New York in 1850 (US Census Bureau, 1850). He was 5'7" with blue eyes and dark hair. George enlisted in the company as a private on October 16, 1861. He fell ill and was moved to Carver Hospital in Washington D.C. He was made a corporal in July of 1862, but was discharged later that year in October for disability. Afterwards he served with the 51st NYS Militia for 30 days and then the 14th New York Heavy Artillery as a Sergeant. George had moved to St. Lawrence, New York by 1863 with his wife Sarah Wilson, and was recruited from DePeyster into Company I. From there he was ordered to Fort Richmond in the New York harbor.

The 14th was at Peterburg, a majority of the companies were at Fort Steadman acting as infantry, George's company I however was at Fort Haskill with companies K, L and M. This was extremely fortuitous as Fort Stedman was overrun by a last-ditch surprise confederate attack on March 25, of 1865. Many of the 14th were captured or killed. Major Randall, commanding the regiment at Fort Stedman was captured but managed to get away and find his way to Fort Haskell. By this time the garrison was well aware that Stedman had fallen and were waiting for the Rebels to advance on Haskell. As the line appeared, Captain Houghton, in charge of the 14th at Haskell ordered his cannons to open fire, which stunted the initial charge. Houghton was severely wounded, but at that time Major Randall had arrived to take command. Subsequent charges on all sides of the fort were stopped as well. He was mustered out of the heavy artillery July of 1865.

George, a physician post-war, applied for a pension in 1880. Also 1880 his sister-in-law Florence Wilson, who was a school teacher, had moved in with George and Sarah (US Census Bureau, 1880). On the 1890 veteran schedules George was complaining of heart disease. He never fully recovered from the illness suffered during the war and had to stop practicing medicine after a period of time. His wife, Sarah passed in 1892 and George lived alone afterward (Brasher Falls, 1896). He passed in May of 1896 and was buried in the Fairview Cemetery in Brasher Falls, St. Lawrence.

Frederick C. Hartmann

Frederick Hartmann, a porter born in Germany, was one of the initial recruits for the sharpshooters; he was 24 when he enlisted at the Montague St. office on September 5, 1861. Often misspelled Hartman, he was appointed a corporal on October 8th 1862 and was discharged nine days later. Frederick was sick in April of 1862 and sent to the US General Hospital. He was detailed on special service shortly thereafter.

He returned home to his wife Mary and six children and became a police officer. Their property was valued at $3000 in 1870 (US Census Bureau, 1870). Frederick applied for, and received a pension in 1881.

Edwin H Lynde

Edwin was enlisted in Willsboro, NY at the age of 20. His parents, Denny and Adelia were farmers from Willsboro, New York. In 1860, also living with the family were Edwin's sister Alois and grandmother Ermin as well as Lucy Bowey who was listed as a servant. Harry, an older brother, had already moved out. At that time, the property was valued at $5,000 (US Census Bureau, 1860). Edwin was descendent of Jonathan Lynde who was a private in Massachusetts and was wounded during the battle of Bunker Hill during the Revolution (Tousley, 1968).

Edwin entered the service on November 7, 1861 and he was promoted to corporal in July of 1862. He reported to the Auger General Hospital in Alexandria, VA, in May 1864 but returned to the ranks by June. Edwin transferred with the company to Company D and was discharged October 9th 1864.

He had moved to Iowa by 1870 where he worked as a farmer and lived with his wife Ann Lincoln, who was also from New York, and their six children (US Census Bureau, 1870). Edwin passed in May of 1903 and is buried at the Crystal Cemetery in Tama, Iowa.

Martin V. Nichols

Martin was born August 28, 1841 in Essex, New York, to farmers Aaron Nichols and Hannah Boutwell. They lived in Willsboro with Martin and his five siblings; Eleanor, Sabria, Cassius, Emma and George. Aaron had been born in Vermont June 26 1817; he passed in May of 1886. Hannah was born in Connecticut in 1820 and lived until 1909. Martin was 19 at the time of enlistment on November 10, 1861. He was captured at Seven Days Battle, and was cited for bravery at Gettysburg. He was promoted to corporal April 19th, 1864, but was captured less than a month later during the Wilderness campaign. Nichols and Doty were sent to Andersonville prison. Both survived the terrible conditions there.

In 1864, Martin moved to Sombra Springs, Ontario where he was a delivery man for a grocer and later, a farmer (Library and Archives of Canada, 2004). He was married to Catherine Nichols. After Catherine passed, he married Aurilla Reece on October 15th 1903 (Ancestry.com). He passed August 22nd 1908 and Aurilla applied for, and received a pension.

Nathaniel Rouse

Nathaniel was born in Columbia, NY October, 17 1838 to Phillip and Jane Rouse. They were farmers living in Germantown in the 1850's, where their property was valued at $1,500. He had three brothers, Alonso, Charles and Philip (US Census Bureau, 1850).

They were descendent of Johann Kaspar Rausch who settled from Germany to Albany in 1709. Nathaniel's father served as a school commissioner for Germantown in Columbia County (Ellis F. , 1878).

Nathaniel was recruited from Fishkill, on September 25, 1861, and was promoted to Corporal in shortly thereafter. On his muster roll card and the 1850 census he is written as Matthew. He took ill at Falmouth and died of typhoid fever Christmas Eve, 1862. He is buried at the Fredericksburg and Spotsylvania National Military Park.

Isaac Smith

Isaac was 25 years old when he was recruited from Babylon, New York on September 17, 1861. He was from Stony Brook, New York and was a sailor prior to the war. According to a muster roll abstract from the 124th New York, he was 5'6" and had blue eyes and brown hair. He was promoted to corporal and transferred with the company to Company D. He re-enlisted in 1864 and was transferred with the others to Company K. What was left was then transferred to Company C of the 2nd US Sharpshooters, then to Company H of the 124th New York then to the 93rd New York. He was mustered out in September of 1865.

In 1880 Isaac was working as a clerk in a store and living in Brooklyn, New York with his wife Annie and their children Charles and Sarah (US Census Bureau, 1880). Isaac Smith had a terrible fate befall his family in December of 1904. Isaac had moved with his daughter, son-in-law and their children to Williamsburg, New York. On the night of the 17th, Arden Reynolds, a lodger was bringing an oil heater to the apartments located in the upstairs of 184 South 9th St. when the heater exploded. The house caught fire quickly and Reynolds, Isaac's grandson Charles Paynter and another lodger Alice Swinson were killed. Isaac was severely injured as was his daughter Sarah Paynter. Sarah had fallen along with her baby and two firemen when the ladder rescuing them broke. Her husband A. Lincoln and Isaac's son Charles were unharmed as was her three day old baby (Three dead, seven hurt in Williamsburg Fire, 1904). It was shortly after that in December of 1907 that Isaac was admitted into the Soldier's Home at Bath. He passed of bronchial pneumonia on December 23, 1909 while at the home.

Ezra Soper

Ezra was the son of John Soper and Lavinia Totten. The Soper's were farmers whose property was valued at $1,400 in 1850. Ezra had four siblings; William, Elbert, Adrianna and John (US Census Bureau, 1850). Their ancestor Henry Soper was born in Southampton, England. His son, Benjamin owned land in Crab Meadow.

Soper was a 22 year old carpenter from Babylon when he passed the initial test on August 26, 1861. Ezra was quickly promoted to corporal in October of 1861. He was returned to New York in 1862 on sick leave, but returned to the company and was mustered out in September of 1864. After the war he worked as a house carpenter, marrying Julia Oakes in 1867 and having two children Sadie and Lottie (US Census Bureau, 1900). Later in life he moved in with his son-in-law George Powell who was living in Amityville on Sammis Ave. Ezra was active in the William Guerney post 538. Amazingly his father John lived to the age of 94 and passed in 1903. Ezra succumbed to consumption and passed in February of 1904 and is buried in the Babylon Rural Cemetery. He was survived by his widow and five daughters (Babylon Local Record, 1904).

George W. Wiggins

George was born in 1835, and he enlisted on September 9, 1861. Wiggins was promoted to Corporal and was wounded in 1862 and again at Po River in May of 1864. He was mustered out with the company in September of 1864.

After the war George was married to Isabella Travis, they moved to Marion, Indiana where he worked as a Tinner where they lived with their son Wallis, and Isabella's parents Alfred and Sara (US Census Bureau, 1880). She filed for a widow's pension in 1890, however it doesn't appear that it was granted.

Privates

Charles Henry Ackerman

Charles was born in 1841 to farmers Elias Dobb and Catherine Ackerman. They lived in Newburgh and later Nyack, New York. Charles was descended from Abraham Ackerman and Aeltje Van Leer who landed in Brooklyn in 1662. The Ackermans and the Browers are cousins (Chester, 2013). Charles enlisted in the Berdans at the age of 20 on November 21,

1861, and was wounded at Harper's Ferry in 1862.

He was discharged in November for disability. He later served with the 16th New York Cavalry but was listed as a deserter August of 1865, he however was transferred due to consolidation to the 3rd New York Provisional cavalry in August and was mustered out in September of 1865. He is incorrectly noted as George on his muster roll, which probably accounts for the confusion. Further evidence that he was not a deserter comes when Charles applied for and was granted a pension in 1874.

Charles married Ruth Barton and they had one daughter, Henrietta. He passed August 10th 1913 at his home in Monsey, New York.

Thomas Andrews

Andrews was born in 1838 to John and Mary Andrews, who had emigrated from Scotland. John was a clerk, and the Andrews family lived in Brooklyn. He served with the 21st Pennsylvania Infantry prior to the sharpshooters call for enlistments. The 21st was mustered into service April 20th and were mustered out in August of 1861. During that time, the 21st crossed the Potomac, advanced on Bunker Hill and marched towards Harper's Ferry before mustering out. Shortly thereafter, on September 5th Thomas enlisted in the sharpshooters. He mustered out with Company H in September of 1864 and went on to marry Caroline Hadenkemp and have three children: Fred, Mary and Hatti.

Thomas worked as a dry goods merchant in New York, and passed November 18, 1906. Caroline filed a widow's pension request in 1906. Thomas, Caroline and Frederick are buried at the Cedar Grove Cemetery in Flushing.

John Bala

John was born in 1831 in Chenango, New York. He was 5'8" had blue eyes and dark hair. By 1860 he was living with his wife Annie, and their children William, David, Mary and John in Newport, New York (US Census Bureau, 1860). He listed his employment as laborer on the 1860 census, but farmer on his muster papers in September 1862. His name frequently shows up as Bela on muster forms. He was only in the company a short time before being discharged in March of 1863 on account of frostbite in his feet (Provost Marshal General's Bureau).

John passed in May of 1888 in Herkimer. He is buried in the Oak Hill Cemetery. In 1888 his second wife Catherine filed a widow's pension request.

George M. Barber

George was born in May of 1841 in Potter, Yates, New York to Culver and Charlotte. According to the 1860 census Cluver's property was worth $3,645 and his personal estate was $2,023. They were predominately farmers, though George's older brother Jeremiah was a teacher. George had five other siblings: Theodore, Catherine, Miles, Melvina and Ella Jane (US Census Bureau, 1860).

He enlisted in Company B of the 1st US Sharpshooters and was transferred to Company H on November 5, 1861. He was wounded at Second Bull Run, for which he would be discharged from the army from Elmira in December of 1862. George applied for a pension in February of 1863.

After the war, George attended the Eclectic Medical Institute in Cincinnati, Ohio and would become a surgeon. He married Mary J. Haines. They would have two children: William and Miles. George passed in September 4, 1888 at the age of 49 and is buried in the Benton Rural Cemetery in Yates, New York. His son William was also a doctor, having studied at NYU, and at the Miami Medical College in Cincinnati.

Edward A. Barto

Edward was born to William and Mary Barto in 1840. Descendent from the Barteau line stretch back to France, it is quite possible that the first Barto in the US was probably John Barto, who settled in Flushing Queens near 1670. William was a carpenter from Huntington, with property valued at $900 (US Census Bureau, 1850). Edward lived with his parents and sisters Mary, Caroline and Emma. Prior to his service in Company H, Edward (incorrectly written as Edmund) was working as a farm laborer (US Census Bureau, 1860).

When Edward mustered into company H, on August 26, 1861, his name was incorrectly written as Barton. In July of 1862 he was wounded in the foot and was sent to the general US Hospital from where he was discharged from the army in October of 1862.

Edward never fully recovered and passed in 1869. He left behind a widow, Annie A Scofield and a son, Willie. They were able to apply for, and receive pensions. Edward Barto is buried in the Babylon Rural Cemetery.

John M Baylis

John was born to John and Susan Dow. John Baylis Sr. had been born in Patterson NJ, and had 10 children with Susan. At age 18 John Jr. left Islip for a short naval career including trips to Charleston and the West Indies. He was 24 when he was enlisted in Company H, on August 31, 1861, and was working as a boatman in Babylon. His service would be cut short in September of 1862 due to asthma.

After his discharge, he returned to his native Babylon and purchased a coast wrecking vessel for working on the south shore of Long Island. His first wife Annie Mallard passed in 1867, His second wife Louisa lived until 1928. John had four children: Richard, Katie, Florence and Edward. In 1875 John left the sea faring business for work as a hotel manager and owner, as well as a restaurant owner until his death in 1906. He owned and operated a hotel on Fire Island for 10 years, after which he returned to Babylon to open a boarding house. He was a member of the William Guerney Post 538 of the GAR.

John was the last surviving member of the Babylon Sharpshooters (Babylon Local Record, 1904). John applied for a pension in 1891 and his widow applied for a pension in 1906. He is buried at the Babylon Rural Cemetery.

Ramsey Black

Ramsey was born in 1834 and was a clerk from New York prior to the war. He enlisted on September 18, 1861 and served as the company cook. He was detailed for duty at the Regimental Hospital on November 29, 1861. At one point in Frederick Peet's memoirs, Peet mentions that in reading the death notices of a person named Black, it meant that perhaps Ramsey's son was killed in action

Ramsey himself fell ill and died of consumption August 20th 1862, he was buried in the Greenwood Cemetery in Brooklyn. His death certificate from Pennsylvania reads August 26th (Pennsylvania, Philadelphia City Death Certificates, 1803–1915, 2008).

Richard Lansing Boyd

Richard Lansing Boyd was born in 1842, to Bayard and Manette. Bayard was a paymaster with the Railroad, and the Boyd family property in Oswego was valued at $500. Richard lived with his mother, father, five siblings and two Irish servants (US Census Bureau, 1860). Richard was a descendent of Robert Boyd of Orange County. Robert was lawyer, and had left England for the Colonies in by the Mid 1700's. Robert was appointed to the Committee of Safety for Ulster County during the Revolution and charged with purchasing muskets for the local militias and paying enlistment bonuses to raise troops (Ellis M. , 1915). Boyd enlisted November 7, 1861 from Oswego. Richard was shot in the head June of 1862, and by November of 1863 was transferred to the 16th Regiment, 2nd Battalion, Invalid Corps. From there he was, in April of 1864, commissioned a 1st Lieutenant in the 39th Colored Troops.

By May 1st, he was in command of the company. He was absent sick in the hospital on May 5th and returned to the regiment in June. The 39th participated in the Mine Explosion at Petersburg on June 30th. They were able to skirt around the mass of bodies in the crater and start sweeping trenches in order to make way for a Union charge that never happened. He was placed under arrest on September 20th, 1864, and faced a courts martial for absence without official leave and conduct prejudicial to "good order and military conduct." He was forced to turn over six months' worth of pay.

Richard went home to Oswego on November 24th at the request of his sister. Their father had passed, the family business was in trouble, and their mother's health was ailing. The lawyer handling the business also requested that Richard return home to help sort out some of the issues. Boyd was not granted the 15 day pass but had returned in December. His pay was again stopped by a courts martial. He was ordered to appear before a board of inquiry to assess his ability to perform as a lieutenant; his commanding officer stated he had little value to the regiment. Richard was never seen before the board as he was either in combat or on leave during the examination period.

Richard however felt that his duty to his sick wife was more important, and in fact had attempted to resign before, however his company was in constant combat. On May 29th General Grant wrote that Boyd should be honorably discharged. His resignation was accepted on June 3rd, 1865, however he was not given a final payment as he still owed for the courts martial sentence. By 1880, Richard had moved Marion, Indianapolis with his wife Caroline Mather, their two daughters Carrie and Manetta and their son Frederick. He belonged to the Phil Sheridan GAR Post 615, and was working as a grain merchant. In 1900 they moved to Cook County, Illinois where he died May 5, 1905. He is buried in the Forest Home Cemetery.

John Felter Brower

John was born May 1, 1836, to Hannah Demarest and Abraham Brower. Descendent Adam Brouwer of Germany, his grandfather Abraham and his great grandfather Uldrick served in the Revolutionary War; both were enlisted in Gilbert Cooper's Second Regiment of Orange County Militia. John's Father Abraham died in 1860 while John was living in Rockland County with his sister Rebecca. He was working as a farmer and their property was valued at $4000 (US Census Bureau, 1860).

On his muster abstract, the last two letters of his name were written so close together that his paperwork was filed under Brown instead of Brower. He enlisted on October 1, 1861 at Newburg, New York. He was wounded in the foot but returned to action. He was absent on sick leave from April 1862 through July 1862 and May 3, 1864 to June 30, 1864 until cancelled by a court martial. John was ordered to surrender $30 of his pay for the 1862 sick leave and $10 of his pay for 1864. He was assigned to Fort Hamilton in November of 1862 on attached duty, and again in May of 1863 both on order of Brigadier General H. Brown. He was transferred to Company D in September of 1864 and finally discharged November of 1864. John filed for a pension in January of 1891.

John was a member of the GAR post 590 in Yonkers. At that time he was working as a painter, He died in Yonkers, New York on April 11, 1920.

Andrew Jackson Burr

Andrew was born in 1829 in Bayshore, New York to Joel Burr and Matsey Sammis. Their ancestor Benjamin landed in America before 1635 and was one of the founders of Hartford. Benjamin also fought in the Pequot War (Behling). Benjamin's grandson Joseph moved to Huntington in the early 1700's, he may have also fought in the French and Indian War. Andrew's great-grandfather Isaac (Joseph's grandson) was owner of a large farm, and overseer of highways (Howell, 2009). Andrew was incorrectly listed on the 1850 census as Anson, but was working as a mariner along with his brother Edward. Joel was listed as a fisherman whose property was worth $1100 (US Census Bureau, 1850). Although not popular to discuss, a separate branch of the Burr family arrived with the Winthrop's in 1630. Jehu Burr, settled in Roxbury Massachusetts before settling in Fairfield Connecticut (Todd, 1878). Jehu's descendent Aaron Burr had fought in the revolution, served in many important political positions including Vice President, however a duel and the subsequent killing of the ever-popular Alexander Hamilton resulted in the disgrace of Aaron Burr and the distancing of the Long Island Burr family from that legacy (Ketcham, 1992)

Andrew listed himself as a carpenter prior to enlisting on September 23,

1861. He received a disability discharge in October of 1862 after having part of his right forefinger shot off in June of that year.

After the war he married Lucinda Rhodes, and worked as an insurer and overseer of the poor for Islip. Lucinda passed in 1873. In 1889 Andrew lost an arm to an infection from a nail (Bay Shore Topics, 1889). Andrew who was living in Amityville at the time was nominated for the role of Member of Assembly in Suffolk county in 1896 (Democratic Nominations, 1896). This was shortly after he, his wife Deborah and a few guests had escaped death when a lightning bolt struck the house in July (Terrific Storm, 1896). Deborah herself was struck by lightning the following year, and had been unconscious, but recovered (Damaged by Lightning in Bayshore, 1897). Deborah and Andrew's daughter Grace died of consumption in September of 1898 (Commack, 1898). Andrew remained involved with the Grand Army of the Republic, in the William Garney Post, the same post where Eliphalet Hill served as a Junior Vice Commander. Andrew held a role as quartermaster (Bayshore, 1904). The family moved from Commack to Kings Park in 1910 (Commack, 1910). Andrew died from an infection June 22, 1912 and is buried in Oakwood Cemetery in Bayshore. Deborah passed in 1917; they were survived by their five children: Elmey, Susan, Minnie, George and Anna.

William Henry Burroughs

William was 34 when he enlisted in December of 1861 at New York City. His name on the muster roll has poor handwriting near his initials, and his is listed as William ST Burroughs. He remained with the company through the transfer to Company D, after which he was promoted to Sergeant on November 9, 1864. Shortly after his promotion, on November 22, 1864 he was fully discharged.

He applied for, and received a pension in April of 1893.

Henry Burtless

Burtless was a 22 year old, Seneca Falls farmer at the time of his enlistment on December 5, 1861. His parents, William and Mary operated a farm that was valued at $9500 in 1860 (US Census Bureau, 1860). He lived with his sisters Phoebe and brothers John and Charles. His name on the muster roll is written as Burttess. The fighting at Nelson's Farm was intense and Henry walked away from the line. He was described by Peet as having a long flowing beard and was listed as a deserter June 30th 1862 (Peet F. T., Personal Experiences in the Civil War, 1905).

George Campbell

George was recruited for Company B from the Albany area as a sergeant. George had been born In Connecticut and was a fire smith prior to the war.

James Campbell

James was 22 when he enlisted at Babylon. Prior to the war he was living in Newtown, which comprised five towns in Queens, New York (HISTORY OF QUEENS COUNTY: with illustrations, Portraits & Sketches of Prominent Families and Individuals., 1882). In June of 1862 he was sent to the General Hospital in Newport News as a result of being sick at Gaines Mills. He returned to the ranks in June of 1862 and in November of 1862 he was discharged due to disability from Warrenston, VA.

John B. Chambers

John was born in 1832 in Ontario, Canada. Canandaigua, New York, was working as a mechanic, and living in Babylon, New York when he enlisted in September of 1862. He was 5'6" with grey eyes and brown hair. John was in the company less than four months before he was discharged for disability from Philadelphia, PA.

By July of 1863, he had moved to Russia, New York and was married. The 1880 census reflected a move to De Peyster, St. Lawerence with his wife

Elizabeth, daughters Fannie, Agnes and Prusilla, and sons John, Will and Ken.

Henry C Chasmar Jr

Henry Chasmar, sometimes written as Chasmer, was born in New Jersey in 1843. His parents were immigrants; his father Henry from England, and his mother Margaret from Ireland[37]. They had six children, counting Henry Jr., all born in New Jersey. Henry Sr. worked as a miller and his property was valued at $2,600 (US Census Bureau, 1850). Henry was 18 when he enlisted in New York City. He was discharged for disability from Sharpsburg, MD in October of 1862.

After the war he moved in with his brother John in Bergen, where he worked as a Constable (US Census Bureau, 1880). He applied for, and received a pension in 1890 while living in New York. By 1900 he had moved to Norwalk, Connecticut and was living there with his wife Eunice and two children Lavina and Charles. Henry was working as a bookkeeper and Lavina as a schoolteacher, Charles was a dentist (US Census Bureau, 1900). Eunice passed in 1920 and Henry in February of 1923 at the age of 82.

William A. Conklin

William was a 20 years old when he enlisted. William, also spelled Conklyn on the muster rolls, was sent sick to the US General Hospital after Gaines Mill in June of 1862. He was sent to the US General Hospital again in August of 1862 from Harrison's Landing. In May of 1864, he returned to the US General Hospital, which was stopped by a courts martial and William was forced to give up $10.00. He was on an individual muster out roll on September 17, 1864.

After the war he lived in Brooklyn, and worked as a police officer. He

---

[37] On several census reports, Henry changes the locations of where his parents were born. Often the father was listed as English or Irish. The mother was listed as being born in Ireland, Nova Scotia and New Jersey.

joined GAR post 399 in 1884. Later William would move to Highlands, New York and later Newark, New Jersey, where he lived with Mary Vanote (US Census Bureau, 1910). However by 1920 the census reflected that he married Mary (US Census Bureau, 1920). William applied for a pension in 1892. He and Mary both passed in 1923. They are buried at Oakwood Cemetery in Monmouth, New Jersey.

John Francis Cooley

John, born November 30, 1842, was the son of James Cooley and Elizabeth Bruen. They were descendent from Samuel Cooley and Anne Prudden.

Samuel had traveled along with John Winthrop to settle in the Massachusetts Bay Colony in May of 1631 taking the oath of the freeman[38]. Later they moved to Milford and took the freeman oath in 1639 (Schenck, 1889).

James was working as a wagon maker at their home in Penn Yan in 1860. John was a painter and his brother Bruen a tinsmith. The value of their property was $700 (US Census Bureau, 1860). He was married to Mary Howe and had a son in 1861, also named John F. Cooley.

Both Bruen and John would enter the service at the outset of the war. Bruen served with the 33rd New York and was wounded at Sharpsburg.

At the time of his enlistment John stood 5'7" with blue eyes and brown hair. He had been recruited by Hastings. John was wounded in the hip at Gaines Mill and was given a discharge for disability July 25th 1862. While mending at home he was asked to train the newly formed 148th New York.

John was also asked to recruit and was able to recruit 35 men to join (Graham, 1926). Once they were ready for combat in September of 1862

---

[38] This was an oath that was taking in Plymouth by any person who had no legal encumbrances, promised not to overthrow the government and defend the commonwealth.

he was given the rank of 1st Lieutenant. He was promoted to captain in March of 1864 and wounded in the side at Cold Harbor. John was promoted to Major in October of 1864. 148th folded into the 24th Army Corps in December of 1864 and John was made major of the Sharpshooters on December 5th (Graham, 1926). The 24th was under fire from a battery near Appomatox Court House on April 9, 1865, when Cooley led the sharpshooters to the house to flush out the remaining Rebels. It would be the last action of the war (Ubaudi, 2001). John was mustered out of service in June 20, 1865. He was brevetted a Lieutenant Colonel of Volunteers in 1868 which was revoked. He went on to have a military career, serving with the 13 US regulars as a 1st Lieutenant and then later with the 22nd US Regulars. Bruen, a prisoner at Andersonville eventually succumbed to the mistreatment and wounds suffered and died in 1875.

He retired from the military in 1869 to become an engineer with the Corning and Sodus Bay Railroad and the Elmira and Ithaca Railroad, all while studying to be an attorney. Although his health was not optimal, he did however in 1870 send a letter to the Adjutant General asking about a commission in the Egyptian Army (Cooley, 1870). In 1880 suffering pain from the gunshot wound, as well as rheumatism, Cooley applied for a pension. John died in October of 1887 at the home of his brother George and is buried in Until the Day Dawns Cemetery in Angelica. His son was an inventor and in 1895 had developed a design for a flying airship, though it never did actually fly.

Charles H. Councler

Charles enlisted in September of 1861 and was discharged a few months later in January of 1862 with a disability from Washington D.C. He had been born in Germany and was a Cabinet Maker prior to the war. Charles was mustered into company G of the 144th New York Volunteers later in 1862 and served the remainder of the war eventually being discharged in 1865 as a private. At final pay, he was listed as being a resident of Prattville County, Greene, NY. Charles' name was written many different ways on various documents. Various spellings include; Concler, Congeler, Conncler, Courdes and Correla. Additionally some documentation has the middle initial of "A."

He was admitted into the Bath Soldiers Home twice for chronic Rheumatism. Stating that he was living in Middletown, Orange, he was admitted in January of 1880 and released at his own request in 1880 and again in February of 1882 and was released in April at his own request. Charles had no listed relations and was single for both entries. According to the history of the 144th New York infantry Charles, with the last name spelled Courdes, was dead by 1903 (McKee, 1903).

Seth M Coutant

Seth was born to Gabriel Coutant and Mary Ferguson and was living in Rosendale, New York prior to enlisting. They were descendants of Jean Coutant, one of the first Huguenot settlers, who was born in France in 1658 and immigrated to the Colony in 1689. In 1710, he was elected assessor for New Rochelle and died in 1717. His grave was twice moved for the construction of interstate highways (Jean Coutant, 2008). Seth was also a descendent of a Revolutionary War veteran on his mother's side. Cornelius Van Wey was a private in the second regiment of the Duchess County Militia (Mellish, 1962).

Seth enlisted in Company H but was discharged less than 5 months later in January of 1862 on a disability from Washington, D.C. On his muster roll his name is written as Constant. He used several names after leaving Company H to enroll in other units. He was also known as Albert Clements and Simon Coulter. He served with the 19th New York Cavalry, 6th New York Heavy Artillery and the 10th New Jersey Infantry. With the 6th NY Heavy Artillery he served with George Ennis, who was in Company G. When Coutant enlisted in the 6th it was actually the 135th Infantry, however they were converted to heavy artillery. With the 6th NY Heavy Artillery he was wounded at Spotsylvania Court House. He was sent to Finley General Hospital in May of 1864 and was absent from the hospital, but returned to duty in July. He was reduced in rank from corporal to private in December of 1864.

After the war he married Mary, and moved to Lasalle, Illinois, where he worked as a carpenter. He applied for a pension in 1892 and was admitted into the Danville Branch of the Soldiers Home in September of 1900 complaining of paralysis. He was discharged in November of 1911 at his own request.

William Winthrop was not the only Company H member with a famous brother who was an author; Seth's brother Charles Griffin Coutant had started as an editor for the New York Sun, settled Topeka, Kansas in March of 1878 and in 1899 had written the History of Wyoming which was published by Chaplin, Spafford and Mathison.

Seth was a member of the Fort Dodge, GAR Post 293, and in 1904 was serving as the Sergeant Major. By 1910 Mary had moved to the Illinois Soldier's Widow's Home in Wilmington (US Census Bureau, 1910). In April of 1915 Seth walked into a Topeka, Kansas police station and confessed of his mass enlistments and desertions. He was described as having a beard that extended to his waist. However the Newspaper believed Seth was suffering from dementia, yet Seth was attempting to clear his conscious. D.D. Laferty of the special inspector for the bureau of pensions. In September of 1915 Coutant was removed from the Soldiers Home in Leavenworth.

George H. Countryman

George was a 35 year old mechanic from Russia, New York. He stood 5'11" with dark eyes and black hair. George was enlisted in August of 1862 and was discharged in March of 1863 from a convalescent camp. He signed his muster roll Webster A. Countryman; however Webster A, also a 35 year old from Russia, New York only lists the 175th New York on his pension record. Further, George had dark eyes and black hair, Webster was blue eyed and brown hair. Both were 5'11" but Webster listed his occupation as a painter as opposed to mechanic. There is no record of either in the census from 1850-1900. However Webster was married to an Eliza and was buried in the Poland Cemetery in Russia, Herkimer.

Michael Curry

Michael was 23 when he enlisted in 1861. He served with the company through muster in September of 1864 although he was ill at Culpepper October 1863. On his muster abstract his name is written Curey.

Henry W. Ecker

Henry was recruited from his home in Alexandria, New York in September of 1862. He was born on October 17th, 1837 to Adam and Alzina. Their farm was valued at $2,500 in 1850 (US Census Bureau, 1850). By 1860 Henry was working as a farm laborer and living on the Weekfield farm in the town of Theresa in Jefferson, New York (US Census Bureau, 1860). He was 5'8" with dark hair. Henry was transferred to company D when H was mustered out, re-enlisted in 1864 and was transferred with the others to Company K. What was left was then transferred to Company C of the 2nd US Sharpshooters, then to Company H of the 124th New York. He was officially out of the army in June of 1865.

He applied for and received a pension in 1890 while living in Kansas with his wife Alice Converse. They had four children Guy, Dietrich, Myrtle and Jurius and worked a farm. Henry died in September of 1903 in Stanley, Kansas. He is buried in the Pleasant Valley Cemetery along with Alice, who had passed in 1901, as well as Myrtle (1900) and Henry Dietrich (1932).

William T. Edgerly

William was 30 when he enlisted in the sharpshooters in September of 1861 atNew York City, and was made a Corporal right away. William was stripped of his rank and transferred to G company just days later. William was in company G until August of 1862 when he deserted.

George A. Ennis

Ennis was from Rockland, New York he was 5'10" with grey eyes and brown hair. He lived in Orangetown with his mother Susan, sisters Mary and Margaret and younger brother Henry. His father Allen was a shoemaker.

When George enlisted in October of 1861 he listed his occupation as shoemaker as well. He was wounded at Harpers Ferry, VA and was discharged in November of 1862. He later served with the 6th New York Heavy Artillery and remained with them throughout the end of the war.

He returned to Rockland and married Sarah A Ten Eyck in 1868 and had three children: Corin, Allin and Wilbert. They lived at 50 Catherine St. in Nyack. In 1882 George transferred from GAR post 82 to GAR post 253. He applied for a pension in 1897 and entered the Roseberg Branch of the Soldiers Home in Virginia complaining of Chronic Rheumatism, defective vision and mitral insufficiency. He left the home in March of 1915. He passed in January of 1916.

John A Fackner

John was a japaner according to his muster roll when he enlisted in September of 1861. He was sick at the West Point, VA hospital in May of 1862. He was transferred to the New York General Hospital where he received a disability discharge in November of 1862. As per a courts martial he was to forfeit $5.00 per month in pay for one year. On his muster roll his name is written Facknoe.

Richard Foster

Richard was 38 when he left his Port Washington home for Company B. Richard had been born in England October 10, 1822 to Richard Foster and Fanny Hines. His father was a lock and gunsmith who passed in 1852 while still living in England. With the knowledge gained from his father, Richard was one of the regiment's armors. Since the Sharp's Rifle was such a unique weapon, they were not repaired by the general federal armories, and therefore the armorers were kept in the regiment[39].

Foster however deserted to Canada from Company B while on furlough and on paper was transferred into Company H in February of 1863 (Skillman, Carey, & White, Who were they? The 1st Regiment U.S.

---

[39] There are a couple of receipts of arms while he was with Company B issued by Caspar Trepp showing Foster as one of the armorers for the Reigment.

Sharpshooter Armorers, 2012).

After the war he moved to Gratiot, Michigan, and had unfortunately lost his foot in an accident. He was married to Elizabeth, and they had seven children. Richard applied for a pension but was denied. He passed May 12, 1909 and is buried in the Collister Cemetery in Gratiot County, Michigan.

Aaron Hall Fuller

Fuller was a married farmer from Saratoga when he enlisted at the age of 34 in 1862. He was wounded at Cold Harbor in 1864, but remained with the regiment. He was transferred to company D when H was mustered out, re-enlisted in 1864 and was transferred with the others to Company K. What was left was then transferred to Company C of the 2nd US Sharpshooters, then to Company H of the 124th New York. He was officially out of the army in June of 1865.

He was married to Catherine Sophia Van Eps, living in Tazwell, Illinois, then later moving to Butler, Kansas. The courts did not allow Aaron to divorce his wife however she died in 1885 (Aaron H Fuller, 2012). He moved with his sons Augustus, Edwin and Henry and daughters Bease, Cynthia and Catherine to Minersville, Oregon where he operated a broom factory and lived until he passed, January 8th, 1900. He was buried in the Masonic Cemetery. Aaron Fuller has living relatives.

William Gillen

William at age 24 had several experiences prior to Company H, he served 30 days with the 12th New York Militia, then enlisted in Company B of the 1st US Sharpshooters. The 12th New York was commanded by Col. Butterfield and spent much of the 90 days in protection of Washington. There were some brief skirmishes with rebel troops near Bunker's Hill, Virginia (Twelfth Regiment, 1866). However there were no casualties. He was transferred into Company H October, 1862 as a Sergeant. He was returned to the ranks and served until August of 1864 when he was returned to Company B by order of Captain John Wilson. In April of 1864 by order of a courts martial he was to forfeit $10.00.

His name is often misspelled Gillan or Gillin. After the war he moved to Ventura County California. He applied for, and received a pension in 1890. On the 1900 census he was living in Hueneme in Ventura County and listed his employment as a pensioner.

William Haggart

William was born in 1824 in Johnstown New York to Daniel and Catherine Haggart. Daniel and his father Daniel emigrated from Scotland near 1782. The Haggart's were living in Fulton, New York on a farm valued at $9,000 (US Census Bureau, 1850). By 1860, he had married Helen Osborn and had three children, Duncan, Andrew and Truman (US Census Bureau, 1860). At William's enlistment in September of 1862, he stood 5'10" and was balding, with blue eyes and listed his profession as a hunter. He was only in the company for two months and was discharged in November of 1862 in Philadelphia, PA for disability, as he was an epileptic.

He returned to Fulton where he and to Helen had four more children: Anny, Margaret and Horace. He lived there until his death in 1899.

Clark Hale

Clark was 22 and living in Keene, New York, and was enlisted in October of 1861 out of Jay, New York. He lived with his mother Betsy, father Noah and five siblings. Noah was listed as a millwright in the 1850 census (US Census Bureau, 1850). He was discharged in July of 1862 by orders of General Porter and applied for a pension in 1863. Clark's brother Noah Jr. enlisted with the 192nd New York in 1865, and was mustered out with the company.

He married Elmore who applied for a widow's pension in 1878.

Joseph TH Hall

According to the 84th New York Muster Roll, Joseph was born in Hatfield, England in 1841 and he was working as a clerk prior to enlistment. He transferred into Company H at the age of 20 in Washington DC, November of 1861. He was discharged from the Sharpshooters in March of 1862 to accept a commission with the 1st Long Island Volunteers. He was transferred to the 27th Company of the 2nd Battalion Veteran Reserve Corps in May of 1864.

After the army he served as a special examiner for the Pension Office. Joseph was specially tasked with finding a pension agent who had been cheating soldiers out of their pensions. During this task, he was not fully reimbursed for his expenses and was summarily dismissed from the pension office after lodging a complaint and actually crossed paths with then head of Civil Service Department, Theodore Roosevelt (Senate, 1898). After leaving the pension service Joseph Hall purchased a quarry, and was elected to Washington D.C. House of Delegates.

He came into conflict with O.S.B. Wall whose house on 7th street was impacted by road construction, using, of course, rocks from Hall's quarry (Sharfstein, 2011). Wall ran against Hall in November of 1871 winning by 82 votes (Journal of the House of Delegates of the District of Columbia Part II, 1872). The work on the roads did not stop despite his loss; however Hall was forced to accept less than his contracted rate for the work done. Hall sued in the District of Columbia for the remainder of what he was owed (Hall v District of Columbia, 1896). Although he would receive some payments he returned to court to retrieve the rest and would unfortunately die before seeing any repayment of the money. His wife Julia continued to seek money back from this issue after his death, appealing to the Senate for relief. Separate from the quarry venture, Hall purchased a stake in a steamboat that would sail on the Potomac in 1877 but had not realized that the purchase was made on a boat whose debts exceeded the value of the boat. He stopped making payments and sued for ownership, however he lost the case (Baldwin v. The E. Morris, 1877).

Joseph, who passed in 1899, is buried with his wife at Arlington National Cemetery.

Horace Edward Hand

Horace was born to Sylvenus and Nancy Hand in October of 1830. The Hand family included Horace's sibling Albion, Mary and Washington. Their property was valued at $4,000 in 1850 (US Census Bureau, 1850). They were farmers, living in Austerliz, New York when Horace left for Washington D.C. to join the Company H, in March of 1862. He was discharged in June of 1862 for wounds in New York City.

He married Hannah Deline, a Canadian, in 1873 while in Lexington Michigan. In 1880 they moved to Jefferson, Nebraska Hannah and Horace had two children: Irving and Nancy (US Census Bureau, 1880). By 1900 they had moved to Port Huron, Michigan and also added Uel, Mary Elva, Albion and George to the family (US Census Bureau, 1900). Hannah passed in 1908. According to his death certificate (which had him incorrectly born in Michigan) he worked as a schoolteacher until his death in January of 1919.

Robert William Helms

Robert was 22 when he enlisted from Essex, New York. His parents were John and Ann, John being born in Scotland. The value of their property in 1850 was $1,800 (US Census Bureau, 1850). He was sick at Gaines Mill and was sent to the US General Hospital at West Point, VA. He was then discharged in September of 1862, for disability from Baltimore Maryland.

He moved to Fayette, Iowa with his wife Arthalinda and children: Lulu and Harley. He worked as a station agent for the railroad. In 1918, a woman named Sarah attempted to collect a widow's pension, however it was not granted. According to the 1910 census, Robert was widowed, and a housekeeper was living with him by the name of Sarah Thompson (US Census Bureau, 1910).

Robert passed on New Year's Eve, 1912 and is buried in the Pleasant Grove Cemetery in Fayette Iowa.

Charles C. Hicks

Charles was born in 1842 and was living in Jericho, New York prior to the war. According to his muster roll, he was a 5'8" farmer with blue eyes. His parents were James Hicks and Hannah Tappen. James had served in Captain James McQueen's Company of New York Militia in the War of 1812. Their farm was valued at $1500 in 1850 (US Census Bureau, 1850). His ancestor, Thomas Hicks, served as a clerk for the town of Hempstead[40], and oversaw a transfer of property in Huntington for George and William's ancestor Richard Lattin in 1666. Thomas was given a 4,000 acre tract of land by Governor Nicholls which created an ongoing dispute as to whether the property was in Great Neck or Flushing. It was finally decided in 1675 that it was indeed Flushing. Hicks would serve as a Judge in 1688. By 1698 he had nine servants living with him. He lived to be about 100 years old. According to the New York Gazette, he had over 300 decedents when he passed (Wolfe, 2013).

He enlisted in the company March, 28th of 1863, joining the company in Falmouth, VA. He was transferred to Company D with the company. He was stationed as a guard at City Point Hospital in October of 1864. He was transferred with the others to Company K. What was left was then transferred to Company C of the 2nd US Sharpshooters, then to Company H of the 124th New York then to the 93rd New York. He was mustered out in September of 1865.

Once out of the war he moved initially to Montana, changing his name to Charles Buckman. He lived briefly in California where he had a son, James. He moved again to Gainbrook, British Columbia, Canada, where he lived until October 1st, 1926. In his obituary it mentioned he worked handling a pack train for hunting expeditions (Civil War Veteran Dies Here Friday, 1926). In the history of Queens, New York, his name is improperly listed as Charles Hecks (HISTORY OF QUEENS COUNTY: with illustrations, Portraits & Sketches of Prominent Families and Individuals., 1882).

---

[40] A position that John D. Acker would later hold.

William R. Hicks

William was 22 when he enlisted in the regiment in October of 1861. He remained with the company through June 18th, 1864 when he was killed in action at Petersburg.

Marvin Hillabrant

Marvin was a 30 year old mechanic from Johnston, Fulton County, New York when he enlisted in September of 1862. Often his name is written as Hildabrant or Hildebrant. He was transferred to Company D with the remainder of Company H. He re-enlisted in 1864 and was transferred with the others to Company K. What was left was then transferred to Company C of the 2nd US Sharpshooters, then to Company H of the 124th New York. Marvin was promoted to corporal after his transfer out of Company H.

After his time in army, Marvin returned to Fulton County, working as a teamster, where he lived with his wife: Hannah Van Alstyne and their children: Hannah, Chauncey, John, Robert, Abraham and Maggie. He complained of chronic rheumatism after the war, but lived until 1906.

Akin Ingersoll Jr.

Akin was married and living in Pawling, working as a carpenter, when he enlisted in October of 1861. He is the son of Timothy Akin and Frances Nancy Banks. Timothy was a shoemaker by trade and had been born in Connecticut. They were descendent of John Ingersoll who had emigrated from England to Huntington in the late 1600's. John owned land in Huntington and was in trouble with the town for violating innkeeper laws. In 1690 he sold the Huntington house and bought a house in Crab Meadow (Avery, 1926). Akin married in 1859 to Mary Brady (US Census Bureau, 1860).

Akin's brothers also enlisted; John with the 4th Heavy Artillery, Cyrus and

Martin with the 44th Infantry. John would be captured at Brandy Station and taken to Libby Prison, where he died (New York, Town Clerks' Registers of Men Who Served in the Civil War, ca 1861-1865). Akin complained of varicose veins while in Maryland in 1861. He was detailed to a convalescent camp by orders of Lt. Col. McKenzie, in February of 1863. He deserted on New Year's Eve of 1863, but returned to the company February of 1864. Because of that, he was forced to stay past muster of the company and was transferred to D, where he was discharged in October of 1864.

He returned to Pawling where he worked as a carpenter and lived with his wife Mary Brady, and several children: Anna, Fanny and Hattie (US Census Bureau, 1870). Mary passed in 1888. Later he moved out to Indiana with his new wife Kate Downs and daughter Fannie, and then on to Los Angeles. He was admitted to the Los Angeles Veteran's Home in 1897. He remained there until he passed on March 17th, 1907 and according to his Veteran's Home record he was buried at the Los Angeles National Cemetery, though he is not listed on the register.

Ebenezer Jones

Ebenezer was living in the 11th Ward of Manhattan[41], with his wife Mary, working as a painter when he was recruited in August of 1861 (US Census Bureau, 1860). He was born to Ebenezer and Isabella in 1831, Ebenezer Sr. was a painter by trade as well (US Census Bureau, 1850). He was discharged in June of 1862 for disability at Gaines Mill. He enlisted in the 1st New York Mounted Rifles August of 1862. He was detailed as the Company Cook. He was charged with desertion in August of 1865 from Fortress Monroe, however that charge was cleared and he was given a discharge as of August 15, 1865.

Although he did not request a pension, his wife Mary filed for a widow's pension in 1892.

---

[41] Today's Lower East Side

Patrick Joyce

Patrick was born in Ireland and was living in Albany when he enlisted into Company B. He transferred to Company H in October of 1862. He deserted the company just after Gettysburg, July 7th of 1863 while the company was at Emmitsburg, Maryland.

John Kenoway

John was one of the oldest members of the company, enlisting at age 43 from his Islip home, where he was married and worked as a baymen. John was of Scottish descent but was actually born at sea. John served until November 22nd, 1862 where he was discharged for disability at the New York City hospital. He had been sent to the NYC General Hospital in charge of the sick from the company. John remained at the hospital to assist.

He returned after the war to his wife Rhoda Furman and they moved to Bayshore, New York not long after. He lived there until his death in November of 1901. He is buried at the Bayshore Oakwood Cemetery.

James Larrason

James was 24 when he left his wife Ann and son Rodolph to serve in Company H. He was wounded at Williamsburg and at Nelson's Farm and was captured May 5th of 1862. James was discharged for disability March 26th 1863. He was employed with Hulse and Begeber in Greenpoint however was so crippled and mentally damaged, he felt that he could no longer provide for his wife and son. On July 28th 1863, suffering from pains related to his wounds and their treatment, he tied a carpet bag filled with stones around his feet and waited for the Greenpoint ferry to be at the middle of its trip. Once there he stepped off of the ferry and drowned. He left a suicide note that was republished in the New York Times (Extraordinary Suicide, 1863).

George Lattin

George joined with his younger brother William from Farmingdale; often both Lattin brothers were referred to as Latting. Their earliest known American descendent was Josiah Letten who was born in 1640 in Massachusetts. It is quite possible that his father Richard was in America and resettled in Huntington soon after. Eventually the family settled in Lattingtown, in Suffolk County. Their father, Henry was born in 1806 in Oyster Bay, their mother Julia Wood was born in Babylon in 1813. They were farmers, and the value of their property was roughly $1,000 (US Census Bureau, 1870).

George was enlisted officially in October of 1861, and remained with the regiment through the transfer to Company D. He was discharged in October of 1864.

He moved after the war to Brooklyn with his wife Emily, who had been born in England, and children Carrie, George and Joseph. George was working as a carpenter (US Census Bureau, 1870). Unfortunately their son Joseph only lived for one year before passing in 1868. An additional tragedy struck the Lattin family in 1868. George and William's sister Susannah died at the private "lying-in" hospital of Dr. H.D. Grindall in Amityville under mysterious circumstances. Their father testified at the inquest that she had visited a brother in Oyster Bay, but never returned home. George testified that he had heard she was destitute and living with a man, George C. Houghton, who had left her and moved to Maryland (Amity-Place Mystery, 1868). It was discovered during the inquest that Susannah had gone to Dr. Grindall for an abortion and died as a result of a post-operative infection, which Dr. Grindall had mistaken for typhoid fever (Daughter of a resident of Farmingdale dies under suspicious circumstances. , 1868). As a result the corner asked to have a law enacted to regulate abortion clinics (The Lattin Case, 1868). George lived in Far Rockaway through April of 1909. There are several living descendants of the Lattin Family.

William H Lattin

William was born on July 10th of 1842 and was just 19 when he enlisted with his older brother George from Farmingdale. William was severely wounded August 30th, 1862, and would be transferred to the invalid corps July 1st, 1863 after he was deemed unfit for duty.

William returned to Oyster Bay after the war with his wife Ella, and had two children: Amy and Attel, however, the years 1868-1874 were very difficult for the Lattin Family. George's son Joseph and Susannah died in 1868; Charles, George and William's brother died in 1869; Amy, William's daughter died in 1870; William and Ella died only months apart in 1871; George and William' mother Julia died in 1873; Attel died at age 7 in 1874. All were buried in Bethpage Cemetery located in Bethpage, New York (Eardeley, 1918)[42].

Sylvester D. Lawson

Sylvester was born April of 1842 to Robert Lawson and Hannah Budd in Poughkeepsie, New York. He was 5'10" tall with blue eyes. Robert was a linen manufacturer who was born in Ireland; Hannah was born in New York. Sylvester had two sisters, Sarah and Caroline and a brother Harry.

Sylvester was enlisted April 30th in Company I of the 71st New York Militia. The 71st left New York in April along with the 6th and the 12th, and was in charge of guarding the Washington Navy Yard upon its arrival in D.C. They would be transferred, however, to Burnside and along with the 69th New York, 14th Brooklyn, and 79th New York who were amassed at Bull Run. The 71st was involved in heavy fighting for most of the day, and retreated as the Confederates attacked across the field. The 71st returned home to New York on July 26th (Person, 2008).

Sylvester then opted to enlist in the sharpshooters. He was wounded in the foot in June of 1862, and was taken prisoner, but returned to service

---

[42] It is worth noting that the transcription has the dates of Attel, William and Ella written as 189- and should all be 187-

with the company. He was transferred to Company D with the company. He re-enlisted in 1864 and was transferred with the others to Company K. What was left was then transferred to Company C of the 2nd US Sharpshooters, then to Company H of the 124th New York. While with the 124th he was promoted to 1st Lieutenant.

During the course of the last few months of the war, Lawson was in command of company I. Shortly after Carmick's death at Boydton Road, and with many of the men starving, Lawson was able to find and kill three large pigs, much to the dismay of a southern miller (Weygant, 1877).

Lawson returned to Orange County after the war to open a store. He married Sallie Borden in 1868. Sylvester lived his wife and five children, Suilla, Robert, Montgomery, Hattie and Carrie. Sallie unfortunately passed in 1880, and Sylvester eventually moved into the Fetter residence as a boarder. He was working as a janitor at the time.

Lawson was admitted and discharged from the Bath Veterans Home several times from 1904-1931.He was admitted with a diagnosis of chronic alcoholism and general disability. Lawson did join GAR post 248 while at the hospital in 1923. He died at 10:40 on June 7 of 1931 suffering from arteriosclerosis. He effects were given to his daughter Hattie Upright, who was living in Highlands, New York. He is buried in the Bath National Cemetery.

George A. Livingston

George was 17 and living in Austerlitz when he enlisted in November of 1861. He fell ill at Gaines Mill in 1862 but remained with the company through the transfer to Company D in 1864. He was discharged in November of 1864.

He married Sarah Ann Park in 1865, and was living in Spencertown, where he worked as a mason. She passed in 1891. In 1901 he married Adeline Slater and they later moved to Kinderhook and finally Chatham, New York. George passed on Independence Day, 1919 and is buried in the Spencertown Cemetery.

Peter Louis

Peter was born in France in 1821 and was living in New York when he enlisted in Company B. His name is written on muster rolls as either Louis or Lewis. He transferred into Company H in October of 1862. Peter was wounded in Hanover in 1862 and sent home. He was dropped from the muster rolls as per G.O. 92 and 102. He was also listed as being sick May 27, 1862, even though he was thought to be well. He would be discharged in August of 1864 for disability from New York City.

He was working as a pattern maker after the war; living in between Broom and Spring streets with his wife Rosalie. The value of their property was $1,000 (US Census Bureau, 1870). Rosalie applied for a widow's pension in 1880.

Sylvester Loomis

Sylvester was 18 when he enlisted and was with the company until March of 1864 when he deserted from his veteran's furlough.

Clinton Loveridge

Born to Cicero and Gloranah (sometimes Lorena) Clinton grew up the son of a well-known and well-respected father. Cicero was a lawyer, editor of the Troy Globe and Mail and Police Justice of the City of Albany. Scarlet fever killed Cicero when he was only 34, in his obituary, Cicero was also described as an excellent orator. After Cicero's death there is not a wealth of information in regards to the Loveridge's until Clinton attended the Albany Free Academy with his older brother Eugene in the 1850's (Bogart, 1852). Their mother Lorena was a school mistress and their sister Jane, a school teacher. Clinton himself was an artist living in Albany when he joined Company B. He was transferred to Company H on paper in October of 1862, but had been seriously wounded at Hanover Courthouse in May of 1862. The wound was so severe that Clinton had to have his leg amputated just above the knee. He was transferred to the Invalid Corps in

April of 1864 where he was promoted to 2nd Lieutenant.

After the war, Clinton moved to Brooklyn where he continued to paint, his work being classified as a Hudson River School artist. Clinton passed in September of 1915 and was buried at the Brooklyn Greenwood Cemetery, however he was buried without a gravestone as there was not enough money in the estate for one. Clinton has living relatives.

Samuel J. Marles

Samuel left home at the age of 26 to enlist in the company. He remained with the company through May of 1862 where he was listed as a deserter.

Harvey Mathews

Harvey was living in Jay, New York prior to his enlistment. He was wounded at Harris House in 1864, and was sent to the General Hospital in Annapolis, Maryland. He returned to Company H by June and remained with the company through the transfer to Company D. On his muster roll abstract for Company D, it listed his hometown as Madison, Wisconsin.

Mathews was discharged in November of 1864. After the war, he moved to San Francisco, California where he was a lumber dealer. He married Katherine and had two children; Ada and Edith they lived at 1514 Hyde. Harvey belonged to George H Thomas Post #2 of the GAR. He passed in April of 1910.

Joseph Mathews

Joseph was born in December of 1837 and was from Canarsie, Kings County. He stood 5'4" and had blue eyes. He was born to Jacob Mathews and Susan White, Jacob was a fisherman. His ancestor William Mathews was born in England, probably in 1870. William married Phebe Reckhow in Albany, New York in 1802. At the time of William's death the Mathews family had relocated to Canarsie.

In 1859 Joseph enlisted in the US Navy for a term of three years and served aboard the Wyancott. He enlisted in the Sharpshooters in October

1861 and was discharged in January of 1862 for disability from Washington D.C., but enlisted later in the local 119th New York. Joseph enlisted in June of 1862, and was mustered in September of 1862. He was detailed as a musician, in March of 1863. He was captured at Gettysburg on July 1st. Joseph was in Libby Prison July of 1863 to August of 1863. In April of 1865 he was arrested and being held at Division Headquarters.

He married Elmira Biggs and lived in Canarsie, New York with his children: Maria, Phoebe, William, Maraheli and Caroline (US Census Bureau, 1880). Joseph entered the Rosenberg Branch of the Veterans Home in 1900 complaining of Rheumatism however he jumped the fence and went AWOL in March of 1901. He re-entered the home in July of 1903 and was forced to work 30 days with no pay as part of his re-admission. Joseph was buried in the Canarsie Cemetery March 24, 1907.

Michael J. Mullen

Michael was 25 when he enlisted from his New York home, in November of 1861. Just after Gettysburg, Michael deserted at Emmitsburg, Maryland.

Theodore Stanwood Nash

Theodore was near 43 years old when he enlisted from his home near Austerlitz, New York in November of 1861. He had been born April 2, 1816 in Gloucester, Massachusetts and married Augusta Williams in 1856. His father Lonson Nash and mother Abigail Lowe stayed residents of Massachusetts; Lonson passing in 1863 and Abigail in 1867. Theodore was discharged in May of 1862 for disability from Philadelphia, Pennsylvania.

After recovering he served with the 30th New York Veterans Regiment. Occasionally Theodore referred to himself as Stanwood, and moved his family to Lincoln California, where he continued to work as a tinsmith. He had two children; Caroline and John. Theodore was a member of the E.D. Baker Post 71 of the GAR located in Newcastle. Theodore passed on January 14, 1898 and was interred in the Grand Army Plot in the Odd Fellows Cemetery.

Joseph P. Newberry

Joseph was living in Russia, New York with his wife Almira when he enlisted in the company in October of 1862. He was working as a laborer and living in a house valued at $400 according to the 1860 census. He was born in 1829 to Samuel Newberry and Mary Vail. He was descendent of Tryal Newbery, who had fought in King Philip's War. He was 5'5" with blue eyes and brown hair. Unfortunately he succumbed to typhoid fever in July of 1863 at Annapolis, Maryland.

His wife was Almira C. was able to receive his pension. He is buried at the Pine Grove cemetery in Herkimer.

William Nichols

William was born in 1840 in Ireland and was recruited from Spencertown. He remained with the Company through September of 1864, when he was transferred with the others to Company D. Once in company D, he was made a Sergeant.

He was discharged in November of 1864, and moved to Kinderhook, New York with his wife Jane Brenner. They moved to Chatham by 1900 where William worked as a farmer (US Census Bureau, 1900). William was a member of the General Logan GAR post. He passed in October of 1911 and is buried in the Chatham Rural Cemetery. Jane passed in 1920.

Noah Olds

Noah was living in Herkimer, working as a laborer, married to Phoebe with their children Alba and Horace when he left home to join Company H (US Census Bureau, 1860). He was shot in the right thigh at Gettysburg, and while convalescing, he went absent from the muster rolls from November of 1863 and was arrested and returned in December of 1863. As a result, he was forced to stay in service until February, 28th 1866. He was considered by Frederick Peet to be one of the best shots in the company.

Once out of the army, he returned to Newport with his wife Phoeba, son

Horace and daughter Almanza, who referred to herself as Manda. They lived with Manda's husband Horace Eames and their children on West Street. He worked as a laborer and carpenter until he passed in January of 1898 from an illness. He is buried in the Newport Baptist Church Cemetery.

David Phelps

David was 18 and working as a carpenter apprentice when he enlisted in November at Spencertown. Phelps was born in Austerlitz, New York on January 1, 1842 to Betsy Phelps, David did not know his father, and Betsy never married. In a letter to the Adjutant General of the State of New York, it listed Phelps' death as occurring on April 5th, 1862 when he was moved to a relief position. An exploding Confederate shell killed him instantly. He is buried in the Yorktown Battlefield Cemetery. Frederick Peet considered him to be a model soldier (Peet F. T., Personal Experiences in the Civil War, 1905). His mother applied for a pension in 1863, stating that she had been dependent on David for income. She was given an $8 per month pension (National Archives and Records Administration, 2008).

Edward P. Pulver

Edward was from Chatham, New York and enlisted at age 25 in company H. He was working as a farm laborer (US Census Bureau, 1860). On his muster roll abstract he is listed as Edwin. He was discharged from the company in December of 1862 for disability from Washington, D.C.

He moved with his wife Adelia Walrath to Wayne, New York after the war, with his son William and a boarder Lillia Taylor (US Census Bureau, 1880). He died August 7, 1882.

George Brinckerhoff Pumpelly

George was born in 1842 to his father George James and mother Susan Isabella. George was a descendent of John Pumpelly who was born in 1727 and served in the French and Indian war, as a member of Rogers

Rangers and was said to have been near General Wolfe when he was killed. John later served in the Revolution (Reynolds, 1911). George's father was attended Yale graduating in 1826, and attended Litchfield law school, graduating in 1828. He was responsible for organizing the Erie Railroad and was Vice-President of the New York State Agricultural Society (Mott, 1921).

George listed his occupation in 1850 as a farmer, though his property was worth $20,000 (US Census Bureau, 1850). The family in 1850 consisted of George, his father and mother, and his siblings; James, Charles, Josiah, Mary, and three servants. Josiah would later become a famous writer and founder of the Huguenot Society of America (Mott, 1921).

George enlisted in 1861 and He served through March of 1862 when he was discharged for disability from Washington D.C. His brother James entered the war as a Lieutenant in the 32nd Wisconsin Infantry.

After being discharged George entered Yale University and attended the Sheffield Scientific School (Roll of Honor, 1865). While at Yale he was a member of the secret science society Berzelius, a member of the Baseball Club, an eating club and crew team (Yale Pot-Pourri, 1865). Finishing his degree, he moved to California where he was in charge of the Silver Peak Mining Company.

He returned in 1874 to Candor, New York with his wife Adelade Woodford and sons William, George and Frederick. In 1900 George and Adelade had a servant, Walter Cronk living the household. George operated a lumber factory until his death in December of 1921. All are buried in the Evergreen Cemetery in Tioga.

Levi Sabine

Levi was 40 when he arrived at Weehawken in October of 1861. He was discharged in December of 1862, for disability at Harper's Ferry, Virginia. Also written Sabine, Levi was a surgeon upon entering service, and was a recruit by Harry D Tyler.

Melanthon Sanders

Melanthon was a 26 year old teamster from Albany when he was recruited by Henry Niles. Melathon's father was from Connecticut, his mother from New York. He was sent to the US General Hospital in Yorktown after Gaines Mills. He was discharged in June of 1862 for disability from Washington D.C.

After the war he moved to Troy, New York with his wife Sarah and their daughter Ella (US Census Bureau, 1870) where he resumed working as a teamster. By 1900 he was widowed and working as a servant in Schenectady.

Theodore Sands

Theodore was a 35 year old laborer from Islip, New York when he enlisted in the military. In 1850 he was married to Ruth, and they had a daughter Hester (US Census Bureau, 1850). He was detached for duty at the US Patent Hospital in 1863, but never arrived and was listed as a deserter in September of 1863.

William H. Seaman

William was 18 and living in Queens New York when he enlisted in September of 1861. He deserted in July of 1863 when he was sent sick to a hospital, but never arrived.

Philip Service

Philip was born to Philip Service and Caroline in Herkimer, New York February 28, 1840. They were farmers and lived on property valued at $1,600. Philip's brother William was born in 1845 (US Census Bureau, 1850).

He deserted the company in November of 1863, but returned in December. Philip was sent sick to the General Hospital at Culpepper in 1863, and also the Division Hospital in September of 1864 and was moved to the US General Hospital Beverly in October of 1864. He was transferred to Company D with the company. He re-enlisted in 1864 and was transferred with the others to Company K. What was left was then transferred to Company C of the 2nd US Sharpshooters, then to Company H of the 124th New York.

After the war he moved to Fairfield, New York with his wife Rachel Comstock and child Burton, where Philip worked as a farmer (US Census Bureau, 1880). He passed in March of 1923 and was buried in the Middleville Cemetery in Fairfield, New York. Rachel applied for a widow's pension in 1923. Philip's name was written as Servis in some places.

Henry P. Shove

Henry was 23 when he enlisted in Company H, but he was only in one month before deserting in October of 1861 while the Company was in Washington, D.C. His name is also written as Shool or Shoul.

George Simmons

George had been born in England in 1829. He and his wife Ellen were living in Herkimer, New York in 1860, working as farmers on property valued at $450 (US Census Bureau, 1860).

Due to chronic diarrhea, he was discharged in February of 1862. Simmons applied for an invalid pension in May of 1863. After the war, George moved to Fairfax, Virginia with his wife Ellen and daughter Alice E where he worked as a farmer (US Census Bureau, 1880). Ellen applied for a widow's pension in 1896 while living in Washington, D.C.

Orrin B. Smith

Orrin was the son of Micah Smith and Betsey Newey. Orrin had nine siblings. In August of 1753, Orrin's great-grandfather Ananias Smith married Elizabeth Swezey, daughter of a prominent local family. Ananias was a revolutionary war veteran who had signed the association papers on May 1775 and served in the 3rd Company under Nathan Rose (Butcher, 1944).

Orrin was well known in camp for making a type of pancake from the hardtack issue. It was so well regarded that his comrades used to steal them as they would come off of the frying pan. In one instance, Orrin spit on the pancakes and then dared any man to take them (Doty O. E.). Known as "O.B." during the war, Orrin was discharged for disability at Harrison's Landing in August of 1862, he was suffering from chronic rheumatism and fever. Later in the war he joined the US Navy and served on the armed transport Savannah.

He returned to Patchogue after the war and worked as a house mover and carpenter, and was known as the "Great American Housemover" (Babylon Local Record, 1893). He married Francis Lyons, and belonged to the Richard Clark GAR Post #210. Orrin passed in May of 1926 and was buried in the Patchogue, Waverly Street Cemetery. There is a monument in Patchogue dedicated to Civil War Soldiers, with Orrin's name inscribed on it.

John Snyder

John was just 19 when he enlisted in the Company. John was sent to the US General Hospital sick from Gaines Mills in June of 1862. He served with the company until May 31th, 1864 when he was shot in the lungs at Tomopotomy, Virginia. He was taken to the Soldier's Home in Washington D.C. where he died of his wounds on July 11th 1864. He was buried at Arlington National Cemetery.

Lewis Hatfield Soule

Soule, a carpenter, left for Company H at age 19 having been recruited by George Hastings. He was wounded twice, once in 1862 and once in the knee in 1863. He was sent sick to the US General Hospital at Newport News in 1862. He was transferred, on paper, to Company D and was transferred with the others to Company K. What was left was then transferred to Company C of the 2nd US Sharpshooters, then to Company H of the 124th New York. He was discharged officially in June of 1865 on an individual muster out. Initially Lewis was marked as a deserter from

Petersburg; however he was actually taken prisoner.

He married Logenia Keyes after the war and had two children, Volney and Edith. They lived in Broome County New York, and later Binghamton, New York where he worked as a mill wright, and an engineer (US Census Bureau, 1870). Lewis was living in Brooklyn when he was admitted into the Johnson City Soldiers Home in 1891 for general disability. Initially he stayed for two years, but was re-admitted in 1897, 1901 and 1906. He died in August of 1918 and was buried in Arlington National Cemetery. Lewis' name is often misspelled Louis.

Frank E Stillman

Frank was just 19 when he enlisted in November of 1861; he took ill with a fever while in Washington D.C. Frank was returned to New York to recover, however he deserted officially May 5th, 1862.

Lewis H Strachan

Lewis was living in Orange County, New York and was 18 when he enlisted in September of 1861. He was the son of James and Amelia Strachan who were both Scottish immigrants. James was a grocer, and Lewis, his older brother James Jr. were clerks. Their younger brothers William and Robert were bookkeepers. They additionally had two younger siblings Jane and John (US Census Bureau, 1860).

Robert and James both served with the 7th Artillery and both were corporals when they were mustered out in 1865. He was discharged in June of 1862 for disability from Fortress Monroe after being sent to the US General Hospital for illness in May of 1862.

After the war he moved to New York City where he worked as a clerk. He was married to Mary and lived at 37, 7th Avenue until his death in July of 1926.

James M. Thorn

James was from Glen Falls, New York and was promoted briefly to corporal in 1862, but was returned to the ranks. James was wounded at Petersburg. He was mustered out of the company in September of 1864. After the war, he worked as a clerk and married Ida. They lived in Saratoga Springs with their children Charlotte, Joseph and Phebe (US Census Bureau, 1870). He was admitted to the Veterans Home in Bath, New York complaining of Rheumatism. He listed himself as a widower in 1909. James passed in October of 1922, and was buried at the Bath National Cemetery. There was a contesting widow on his pension, filed by Cordelia Thorn, however neither she nor Ida were issued a widow's pension.

Erastus Tooker

Erastus was the son of Amos Tooker and Jane Weeks. The Tookers were a mariner family and they lived in Babylon with their six children. Amos' father Abijah Tooker signed the Association Papers while living in Brookhaven on June 8th 1775 (Terwilliger, 1868). Ersastus served as a company cook in 1861. Erastus would be discharged in June of 1862 after having been shot three times. Once in the leg, once in the abdomen, and the third shot removing a finger. He filed for a pension and had to answer to why he was never treated for the leg wound. Having witnessed amputations, Erastus dug the bullet out of his leg with his finger instead.

After the war Erastus would become a merchant and ferry captain, opening the first clam shack on Fire Island. Erastus married Mary Wood and had a son named William. In July of 1895 he nearly came to blows with a minister when the Reverend accused him of leaving people on the beach instead of ferrying them across the bay. Erastus was a member of the Knights of Pythiss. In 1888 Erastus moved his family to Patchogue. Their cottage on Oak Beach Island was destroyed by fire in 1901. Erastus passed in September of 1897 suffering from consumption. He is buried with his wife and son at the Babylon Rural Cemetery. In Babylon there is a Tooker Avenue and a Tooker Elementary School.

Isaac L. Underhill

Isaac was 21, 5'6" with hazel eyes and brown hair. He was a druggist living in Newburgh, and was recruited by Harry D Tyler. On the 1860 census, he was listed as a clerk living with his father William who was a hat dealer. The property was valued at $1,000. He also lived with his mother Elizabeth Lockwood, siblings, William, Charles and a border Jane Lockwood. He deserted in April of 1863 while on a ten day furlough.

John Valleau

John was just 17 when he enlisted in the Company from Au Sable Forks. He was born in Troy, New York, February 1844, to Theodore Valleau and Edda Van Raust. In 1860 he was living with his family, who operated a boarding house in Au Sable Forks (US Census Bureau, 1860). John was probably descendent of Isaiah Valleau who was born in 1638 in France. Isaiah and his wife Susannah Descard settled in New Rochelle, New York.

John had grey eyes and was 5'8" with brown hair. He was wounded in the hip at Nelson's Farm in 1862, and taken prisoner. He was discharged in December of 1862. He applied for a pension immediately in May of 1863 and was mistakenly listed as Vallean.

In January of 1864 he joined the 96th New York Infantry. The 96th was in reserve during the mine explosion at Petersburg. He was promoted to corporal in February of 1865, and sergeant in May, but was returned to the ranks in November of 1865 as the army began to shrink.

After the war he moved with his wife Kate and children Mary, Jane, Lucretia and Eda to Paterson, New Jersey where John worked as a machinist (US Census Bureau, 1880). The family was living at 223 Vine St.

He was admitted to the Bath Soldier's Home in 1909 complaining of pain related to the gunshot wound and a hernia. Catherine had passed at this point, and John was eventually discharged from the home in 1910. He passed in 1917.

George W. Vincent

George was 23 and from Austerlitz, New York, when he joined the Company in November of 1861. George was absent sick during June of 1862, when we was sent to the US General Hospital from Gaines Mill, but had returned to the company in July. He died from typhoid fever in August of 1862. He was buried in the Hampton National Cemetery.

George P. Walters

George was the son of Samuel Walters and Ann Poling. They were descendent of Rudolph Walter who emigrated from Germany in 1729. In 1860 George had taken over the farm from his deceased father, and lived there with his mother, and siblings: Mary, Sarah, John and Richard. The property was valued at $2,000 (US Census Bureau, 1860).

He was discharged from the company, after wounds to his kidney and spine, from the hospitals in New York City in October of 1862.

He returned to farming in Raritan with his wife Cornelia and children: George, Mary, Margaret, Theresa and Peter. He worked as a farmer and belonged to GAR Post #83. He passed in January of 1927 and was buried in the Greenwood Cemetery in Keyport, New Jersey.

Andrew Graham Westervelt

Andrew was born to Cornelius Westervelt and Sarah Graham in Poughkeepsie, New York, November 22, 1826. He was living in California, was 36 years old, 5'9" with black hair and listed his job as a hunter when the war started. He, along with California Joe (Truman Head), made their way back to New York to enlist.

Prior to the trip east he had sold off all of his land and donated the proceeds to the government. His friends raised $300 for his trip back to east. He arrived in Washington D.C. in November of 1862. He was transferred, to Company D with the company and was transferred with the others to Company K. What was left was then transferred to Company

C of the 2nd US Sharpshooters, then to Company H of the 124th New York. He was mustered out in June of 1865.

Andrew returned to California, helping to settle and mine Dog Creek, Shasta, California. Andrew only lived to be 45 and passed April of 1872 and was buried in Sutter County Noyseburg Cemetery.

George Emmet Whitney

George was enlisted at Babylon as a 19 year old in 1861. He was living with Walter Robbins working as a clerk in Huntington. George's family came from England, and settled in Connecticut before 1650. Henry Whitney, who settled in Norwalk, Connecticut, wrote John Winthrop for medical advice about his ailing wife (Phoenix, 1878). The Whitney family moved from Norwalk to Stamford, where George's great-grandfather Darling, enlisted in the American Army in June of 1776 and was discharged in December of 1776 (Whitney, 1922).

George was born in 1842 in Commack, Suffolk County to Darling and Harriet Whitney. Darling was a well-known physician, with a large practice and in 1860 the property was valued at nearly $4,000. Darling went on to serve as a corner for Suffolk County, served on the New York Legislature in 1845 and superintendent of the common schools in Huntington. George had five siblings; including his twin, Edwin Ray and living with the family were three others, including Mary A Brown and Caroline Brown. Darling, George, Edwin and older brother Stanton all served in the Army during the Civil War. Darling was a Brigade Surgeon for the New York State Light Horse Cavalry. Stanton who had moved to Wisconsin served with 24th Wisconsin Infantry. Edwin served with the 2nd New York Light Horse Cavalry. All were unharmed and served to the end of the war (Phoenix, 1878). George was wounded in August of 1862 by a spent shell in the shoulder and remained with the company through July of 1863 when he was transferred to the invalid corps.

He returned to his Oyster Bay home, where he lived until January of 1896. He is buried in the Brookville Cemetery.

Thomas N. Williams

Thomas was 19 when he enlisted, according to census records, his parents were both born in England. He was on sick call at Fortress Monroe in 1862 and would be eventually discharged for disability from Alexandria, Virginia in March of 1863.

After the war he was a harness maker for a stable (US Census Bureau, 1910). He applied for, and received an invalid pension in 1890. He passed in Brooklyn, New York, October 22nd, 1918 and is buried at the Cyprus Hills National Cemetery.

Charles L. Wood

Charles was 27 when he enlisted in 1861, however he was transferred immediately to Company G. He served as a hospital nurse, and was mustered out of service on September 22, 1864. He married Mary after the war and she applied for a widow's pension in 1890.

10 BIBLIOGRAPHY

AUTHORS NOTE

A large amount of information can be gleaned from the muster rolls of troops and the six regimental books housed in the National Archives. Information such as height, weight, hair and eye color, cause of discharge, location of wounding, time spent sick, and location of enlistment are included hereafter from the original books housed at the National Archives. Rather than cite each instance of information taken from this book, it will be cited in the bibliography. Conversely, each instance of an appearance on the US Census is listed to ensure that future researchers can pinpoint the proper page. The muster roll abstracts were collected by the New York State Department of Military Affairs, and are available in their Saratoga, New York location. There were a variety of spellings for the names of the soldiers, as in some cases the spelling was done phonetically. For reference purposes each of the variety of soldier's names is included in the biography section located at the end of the book.

BIBLIOGRAPHY

50 Dollars Reward. (1820, April 11). Edenton Gazzette and North Carolina General Advertiser.

1890 USMA class album, special collections, United States Military Academy Library [Print]. (1890).

Catalogue of the Officers and Students in Yale College 1850-1851. (1850). New Haven: B.L. Hamlen.

Legal Notices. (1853, October 6). New York Daily Times.

Establishment of a Mercantile Library Association . (1857, December 1). Brooklyn Daily Eagle, p. 3.

Mechanics' Fire Insurance Company. (1859, August 2). Brooklyn Daily Eagle, p. 4.

(1861, November 11). Islip Corrector, p. 2.

(1861, November 2). NY Daily Tribune, p. 6.

(1861, July 31st). NY Herald, p. 8.

Berdan Sharpshooters. (1861, November 27). Lowville Journal & Republican, p. 2.

Local and Miscellaneous War News. (1861, September 19). Brooklyn Daily Eagle, p. 2.

(1862, June 4). Albany Evening Journal, p. 1.

(1862, July 7). New York Tribune, p. 1.

(1862, February 28). World, New York, p. 6.

Extraordinary Suicide. (1863, August 4). New York Times.

Roll of Honor. (1865). Yale Literary Magazine, 30, p. 104.

Yale Pot-Pourri. (1865). New Haven: Tuttle, Moorehouse and Taylor.

(1866). Twelfth Regiment . In Third Annual Report of the Bureau of Military Statistics of the State of New York. Albany: C Wendell.

Amity-Place Mystery. (1868, August 30). New York Times.

Daughter of a resident of Farmingdale dies under suspicious circumstances. . (1868, August 29). Brooklyn Daily Eagle.

The Lattin Case. (1868, September 9). New York Times, p. 2.

Journal of the House of Delegates of the District of Columbia Part II. (1872). Washington D.C. : Chronicle Publishing Company .

Baldwin v. The E. Morris. (1877, February 19). Connecticut. Retrieved April 16, 2013, from https://1.next.westlaw.com/Document/If989729653b911d9a99c85a9e6023ffa/View/FullText.html?navigationPath=Search%2Fv3%2Fsearch%2Fresults%2Fnavigation%2Fi0ad705210000013e149052da03fae20f%3FNav%3DCASE%26fragmentIdentifier%3DIf989729653b911d9a99c85a9e6023ffa%2

HISTORY OF QUEENS COUNTY: with illustrations, Portraits & Sketches of Prominent Families and Individuals. (1882). New York: W.W. Munsell & Co.

A Reception at the Newark Hotel. (1886, July 10). Newark Union, p. 1.

Bay Shore Topics. (1889, May 25). Suffolk County News, p. 2.

Babylon Local Record. (1893, April 22). South Side Signal, p. 3.

(1895). Class of 1832. In Bowdoin Library Bulliten (pp. 138-139). Brunswick, ME.

Local News. (1895, December 21). South Side Signal, p. 3.

Brasher Falls. (1896, May 20). NY Currier & Freeman.

Democratic Nominations. (1896, October 9). Suffolk County News, p. 2.

Hall v District of Columbia. (1896, June 22). Washington D.C. Retrieved April 16, 2013, from https://1.next.westlaw.com/Link/Document/FullText?findType=Y&serNum=1800118208&pubNum=289&originationContext=document&transitionType=DocumentItem&contextData=(sc.DocLink)

Terrific Storm. (1896, July 31). Suffolk County News, p. 2.

Damaged by Lightning in Bayshore. (1897, June 18). Suffolk County News, p. 2.

Commack. (1898, September 17). Long Islander, p. 4.

Babylon Local Record. (1904, Februrary 27). South Side Signal, p. 3.

Bayshore. (1904, February 12). Suffolk County News, p. 1.

Three dead, seven hurt in Williamsburg Fire. (1904, December 18). New York Times, p. 8.

Commack. (1910, April 22). Long Islander, p. 6.

Civil War Veteran Dies Here Friday. (1926, October 7). Cranbrook Courier.

1st US Sharpshooters. (1861-1865). Regimental Descriptive Books. Washington D.C.: National Records and Archives Administration.

Jean Coutant. (2008, October 24). Retrieved from Find A Grave: http://www.findagrave.com/cgi-bin/fg.cgi?page=gr&GRid=30817256

Pennsylvania, Philadelphia City Death Certificates, 1803–1915. (2008). Retrieved May 9, 2013, from Ancestry.com: http://search.ancestrylibrary.com/cgi-bin/sse.dll?rank=1&new=1&MSAV=0&msT=1&gss=angs-

g&gsfn=Ramsey&gsln=black&msbdy=1834&msbpn__ftp=new+york&uidh=m23&pcat=ROOT_CATEGORY&h=290026&recoff=5+7&db=FSPhilPADeath&indiv=1

Pennsylvania, Philadelphia City Death Certificates, 1803–1915. (2010). Salt Lake City, Utah. Retrieved April 17, 2013, from http://search.ancestrylibrary.com/cgi-bin/sse.dll?rank=1&new=1&MSAV=0&msT=1&gss=angs-g&gsfn=albert&gsln=barrett&mswpn__ftp=new+york&msbdy=1841&uidh=m23&pcat=ROOT_CATEGORY&h=1074818&recoff=5+7+59&db=FSPhilPADeath&indiv=1

Aaron H Fuller. (2012, August 9). Retrieved April 24, 2013, from Ancestry.com: http://trees.ancestrylibrary.com/tree/24766771/person/1823649686/photo/10?pgnum=1&pg=32816&pgpl=pid%7cpgNum

Ancestor Search. (2013). Retrieved May 23, 2013, from DAR Geneological System: http://services.dar.org/public/dar_research/search_adb/default.cfm?Action=Search&Opt=&Last_Name=Granbery&First_Name=&P_ID=&ServiceState=&BirthState=&DeathState=&SpouseLastName=&SpouseFirstName=&Rank=&Live_County=&Live_City=&Live_District=&Live_State=&Pens

Adcox, J. (2000, Mar 4). G W Vincent. Retrieved Jan 6, 2014, from findagrave.com: http://www.findagrave.com/cgi-bin/fg.cgi?page=gr&GSln=vincent&GSfn=g&GSmn=w&GSbyrel=all&GSdyrel=all&GSob=n&GRid=3095788&df=all&

Alpha Delta Phi. (1870). Catalogue of the Alpha Delta Phi Society. New York: Executive Committee of the Alpha Delta Phi.

Ancestry.com. (n.d.). Ontario, Canada, Marriages, 1801-1928. Retrieved May 21, 2013, from Ancestry.com: http://search.ancestrylibrary.com/cgi-bin/sse.dll?rank=1&new=1&MSAV=0&msT=1&gss=angs-

g&gsfn=martin+v+&gsln=nichols&msbdy=1842&uidh=m23&mssng0=Aurilla&pcat=ROOT_CATEGORY&h=2821055&recoff=7+8+9+32+45+56&db=OntarioMarr1858-1899_ga&indiv=1

Army, U. (1999). The Civil War 1861. Retrieved September 24, 2013, from US Military Bookshelves: http://www.history.army.mil/html/bookshelves/resmat/civil_war/extracts/the_civil_war_1861_(pg_199-221).pdf.

Avery, L. (1926). A genealogy of the Ingersoll family in America, 1629-1925. New York: Grafton Press.

B., K. (2011, Oct 30). John Deverson Acker. Retrieved Jan 1, 2014, from findagrave: http://www.findagrave.com/cgi-bin/fg.cgi?page=gr&GSln=acker&GSfn=john&GSmn=d&GSbyrel=all&GSdyrel=all&GSob=n&GRid=79578982&df=all&

Barrett, A. R. (1907). Modern Banking Methods and Practical Bank Bookkeeping. New York: Bankers Publishing Company.

Barrett, W. (1888). Genealogy of some of the descendants of Thomas Barrett, sen., of Braintree, Mass., 1635. St. Paul, MN: D. Ramaley & Sons.

Behling, S. (n.d.). Benjmain Burr. Retrieved May 9, 2013, from Rootsweb: http://homepages.rootsweb.ancestry.com/~sam/burr/benjamin.html

Benson, D. (2012, Nov 8). Pvt Aaron Hall Fuller. Retrieved Jan 6, 2014, from findagrave.com: http://www.findagrave.com/cgi-bin/fg.cgi?page=gr&GSln=fuller&GSfn=a&GSmn=h&GSbyrel=all&GSdy=1900&GSdyrel=in&GSob=n&GRid=100383442&df=all&

Berdan, H. (1861, October 19). Camp of Instruction. Washington D.C.: National Archives and Records Administration.

Berdan, H. (1861, May 28). Caspar Trepp. Sun.

Berdan, H. (1862, December 17). Camp Near Falmouth VA. Falmouth, VA: National Archives and Records Administration.

Berdan, H. (1862, November 27). Letter to Abraham Lincoln November 27, 1862.

Berdan, H. (1863). Report of Colonel Hiram Berdan, First US Sharpshooters, commanding third brigade #149. Washington, D.C.: Government Printing Office.

Birney, D. (1863). Report of Major General David B. Birney, US Army, commanding First Division #44. Washington, D.C.: Government Printing Office.

Birney, D. (1863). Reports of Major General David B. Birney, US Army, commanding First Divison of, and Third Army Corps #133. Washington, D.C.: Government Printing Office.

Bogart, J. (1852). Annual Catalogue of the Officers and Students of the Albany Academy 1851-1852. Albany: Joel Munsell.

Bosley, B. (2010, April 4). Company B 1st Regiment Sharpshooters (Historical Association). (C. Schnupp, Interviewer)

Buchanan, C. J. (1902). Oration by Lieut. Charles J. Buchanan. In D. Sickles, Final Report on the Gettysburg Battlefield (pp. 1062-1079). Albany, NY: J.B. Lyon Company.

Butcher, J. (1944). Empire State Society of the National Society of the Sons of the American Revolution. Herkimer, New York.

Cady, A. (2011, Apr 14). Joseph T H Hall. Retrieved Jan 6, 2014, from findagrave: http://www.findagrave.com/cgi-bin/fg.cgi?page=gr&GSln=hall&GSfn=joseph&GSbyrel=all&GSdy=1899&GSdyrel=in&GSob=n&GRid=68365695&df=all&

Cengage, G. (2008). West's Encyclopedia of American Law. Farmington Hills, MI: Gale Cengage.

Chester, C. (2013, April 19). Master Index. Retrieved May 8, 2013, from The Brouwer Genealogy Database: http://freepages.genealogy.rootsweb.ancestry.com/~brouwergenealogydata/index.htm

Chuck. (2000, Mar 3). Thomas N Williams. Retrieved Jan 6, 2014, from findagrave.com: http://www.findagrave.com/cgi-bin/fg.cgi?page=gr&GSln=williams&GSfn=thomas&GSmn=n&GSbyrel=all&GSdyrel=all&GSob=n&GRid=2600892&df=all&

Clarke, E. (1862, June 19). Camp Berdan's US Sharpshooters. New Bridge, VA: National Archives and Records Administration.

Collins, B. (2010, Sept 8). Frederick Tomlinson Peet. Retrieved Jan 6, 2014, from Findagrave.com: http://www.findagrave.com/cgi-bin/fg.cgi?page=gr&GSln=peet&GSfn=frederick+&GSbyrel=all&GSdyrel=all&GSob=n&GRid=58387244&df=all&

Cooley, J. (1870, October 1). Letter to Adjutant General.

Corser, E. (1898). A Day with the Confederates. In E. Mason, E. Torrance, & D. Kingsbury, Glimpses of the Nation's Struggle (pp. 364-366). St. Paul, MN: H.L. Collins Co.

DBT. (2011, Apr 20). Joseph P. Newberry. Retrieved Jan 6, 2014, from findagrave: http://www.findagrave.com/cgi-bin/fg.cgi?page=gr&GSln=newberry&GSfn=joseph&GSmn=p&GSbyrel=all&GSdyrel=all&GSob=n&GRid=68695840&df=all&

Doty, E. A. (1897). The Doty-Doten Family in America. Brooklyn.

Doty, O. E. (n.d.). Memories of Orrin E. Doty of Co H 1st Berdans, U.S. Sharpshooters. (K. Harris, Ed.)

Doyle, T. (Ed.). (n.d.). Family:Whitney, Henry (s1615-1673). Retrieved May 8, 2013, from Whitney Research Group: http://wiki.whitneygen.org/wrg/index.php/Family:Whitney,_Henry_(s1615-1673)

Dwight, B. W. (1874). History of the Decendents of John Dwight. New York: John F. Trow and Sons.

Eardeley, W. A. (1918). Extracted from Bethpage & Farmingdale Town of Oyster Bay Queens County, now Nassau CountyLong Island, New York Three Cemeteries, 1832-1898. (J. Devlin, Editor) Retrieved May 7, 2013, from http://dunhamwilcox.net/ny/oyster_bay_ny_cem.htm

Egan, T. (1863). Report of Colonel Thomas W. Egan, Fortieth New York Infantry, commanding Third Brigade #52. Washington, D.C.: Government Printing Office.

Ellis, A. V. (1863). Report of Colonel A. Van Horne Ellis, 124th New York Infantry #163. Washington, D.C.: Government Printing Office.

Ellis, F. (1878). Schools Germantown, Columbia County, New York. Retrieved May 21, 2013, from http://www.usgennet.org/usa/ny/county/columbia/gtown/schools.htm

Ellis, M. (1915). Application for Membership to the Society of the Daughters of the American Revolution. Washington D.C.

Farrell, G. (2002). Lillie Devereux Blake: Retracing a Life Erased. Amherst, MA: University of Massachusetts Press.

Foote, L. (2010). The Gentlemen and the Roughs: Manhood, Honor, and Violence in the Union Army. New York: NYU Press.

Google. (n.d.). Clinton Loveridge. Retrieved Jan 6, 2014, from Google: https://www.google.com/search?q=clinton+loveridge&oq=clinton+loveridge&aqs=chrome..69i57j0l3j69i60.3212j0j4&sourceid=chrome&espv=210&es_sm=93&ie=UTF-8

Graham, R. H. (1926). Yates County Boy's in Blue 1861-1865 Who they are and what they did. Madison, WI: University of Wisconsin.

Grant, U. (1885). Personal Memoirs of US Grant. New York: Charles L. Webster & Co.

H., D. (2012, Dec 12). Richard L Boyd. Retrieved Jan 6, 2014, from findagrave: http://www.findagrave.com/cgi-bin/fg.cgi?page=gr&GSln=boyd&GSfn=richard&GSbyrel=all&GSdy=1905&GSdyrel=in&GSob=n&GRid=102636989&df=all&

Hammill, T. (2011, Apr 8). Andrew G Westervelt. Retrieved Jan 6, 2014, from findagrave.com: http://www.findagrave.com/cgi-bin/fg.cgi?page=gr&GSln=westervelt&GSfn=andrew&GSmn=g&GSbyrel=all&GSdyrel=all&GSob=n&GRid=68083905&df=all&

Hastings, G. (1862, April 12). Letter to Lillie Devereaux April 12, 1862.

Hastings, G. G. (1861, August 19). For the War: Berdan's Regiment of Sharpshooters. Brooklyn Daily Eagle, p. 1.

Hastings, G. G. (1862, May 8). David Phelps. Certificiate to be given to volunteers at the time of their discharge to enable them to receive their pay. Yorktown, VA: War Department.

Hastings, G. G. (1862, November 7). Letter to Lille Devereaux. Lillie Devereux Blake Papers, 1847-1986. St. Louis, MO: Missouri History Museum Archives.

Hastings, G. G. (1862, July 6). Letter to Lillie Devereaux. Lillie Devereux Blake Papers, 1847-1986. St. Louis, MO: Missouri History Museum Archives.

Hastings, G. G. (1862, September 5). Letter to Lillie Devereaux. Lillie Devereux Blake Papers, 1847-1986. St. Louis, MO: Missouri History Museum Archives.

Hastings, G. G. (1862, December 25). Letter to Lillie Devereaux. Lillie Devereux Blake Papers, 1847-1986. St. Louis, MO: Missouri History Museum Archives .

Hastings, G. G. (1862). Report of Captain George Hastings, First US Sharpshooters of Operations June 29-July 1 #114. Washington D.C.: Government Printing Office.

Hastings, G. G. (1863, November 19). Letter to Lillie Devereaux. Lillie Devereux Blake Papers, 1847-1986. St. Louis, MO: Missouri History Museum Archives.

Hastings, G. G. (1863, September 20). Letter to Lillie Devereaux. Lillie Devereux Blake Papers, 1847-1986. St. Louis, MO: Missouri History Museum Archives.

Hastings, G. G. (1863, July 28). Letter to Lillie Devereaux. Lillie Devereux Blake Papers, 1847-1986. St. Louis, MO: Missouri History Museum Archives.

Hastings, G. G. (1863, May 5). Letter to Lillie Devereaux. Lillie Devereux Blake Papers, 1847-1986 . St. Louis, MO: Missouri History Museum Archives.

Hastings, G. G. (1863, March 4). Letter to Lillie Devereaux. Lillie Devereux Blake Papers, 1847-1986 . St. Louis, MO: Missouri History Museum Archives.

Hastings, G. G. (1863, December 12). Letter to Lillie Devereaux . Lillie Devereux Blake Papers, 1847-1986. St. Louis, MO: Missouri History Museum Archives.

Hastings, G. G. (1863, June 22). Letter to Lillie Devereaux . Lillie Devereux Blake Papers, 1847-1986. St. Louis, MO: Missouri History Museum Archives.

Hays, P. (2010, Aug 17). Pvt. Lewis H Soule. Retrieved Jan 6, 2014, from findagrave: http://www.findagrave.com/cgi-bin/fg.cgi?page=gr&GSln=soule&GSfn=lewis&GSbyrel=all&GSdyrel=all&GSob=n&GRid=57194246&df=all&

Hooker, J. (1866). Letter to Edward M. Stanton. New York.

Hope. (2009, Aug 18). Pvt. John Snyder. Retrieved Jan 6, 2014, from findagrave: http://www.findagrave.com/cgi-bin/fg.cgi?page=gr&GSln=snyder&GSfn=john&GSbyrel=all&GSdy=1864

&GSdyrel=in&GSob=n&GRid=40826418&df=all&

Howell, C. (2009, December 13). Issac Burr. Retrieved May 9, 2013, from Ancestry.com: http://trees.ancestrylibrary.com/tree/4551480/person/48278664/media/1?pgnum=1&pg=0&pgpl=pid%7cpgNum

Hulbert, C. (1950). Virginia Society of the National Society Sons of the American Revolution.

Hurd, D. H. (1880). History of Clinton and Franklin Counties, New York. Philadelphia: J.W. Lewis & Co.

Isler, J. B. (1889). Report of Captain John B. Isler, First U.S. Sharpshooters of skirmish at Blackford's or Boteler's Ford. In Index to the Miscellaneous Documents of the House of Representatives (p. 345). Washington D.C.: Government Printing Office.

Jones, S. (1891). New York Superior Court Reports. New York: Banks & Brothers, Law Publishers.

Kastenberg, J. (2009). Blackstone of Military Law. Latham, MD: Scarecrow Press.

Kat. (2004, May 25). William A Conklin. Retrieved Jan 6, 2014, from findagrave: http://www.findagrave.com/cgi-bin/fg.cgi?page=gr&GSln=conklin&GSfn=william&GSbyrel=all&GSdy=1923&GSdyrel=in&GSob=n&GRid=8828583&df=all&

Kat. (2007, Jan 6). George P Walters. Retrieved Jan 6, 2014, from findagrave.com: http://www.findagrave.com/cgi-bin/fg.cgi?page=gr&GSln=walters&GSfn=george&GSmn=p&GSbyrel=all&GSdyrel=all&GSob=n&GRid=17326690&df=all&

Kenney, E. (2013, Jun 24). George M Barber. Retrieved Jan 6, 2014, from findagrave: http://www.findagrave.com/cgi-bin/fg.cgi?page=gr&GSln=barber&GSfn=george&GSmn=m&GSbyrel=all&GSdyrel=all&GSob=n&GRid=112816126&df=all&

Laer, A. J. (1908). Settlers of Rennsselaerswyck, 1630-1658.

Library and Archives of Canada. (2004, September 7). Census of Canada 1901. Retrieved May 21, 2013, from Library and Archives of Canada: http://www.collectionscanada.gc.ca/databases/census-1901/001013-119.03-e.php?sisn_id_nbr=4160&page_id_nbr=33397&interval=80&PHPSESSID=epm2rjpe22i930cku73idnb6v6

Lonn, E. (1928). Desertions in the Union Army. Gloucester, MA: American Historical Association.

MacIntyre, K. (2010, Apr 1). William Haggart. Retrieved Jan 6, 2014, from findagrave.com: http://www.findagrave.com/cgi-bin/fg.cgi?page=gr&GSln=haggart&GSfn=william&GSbyrel=all&GSdyrel=all&GSob=n&GRid=50548549&df=all&

McKee, J. H. (1903). Back in the war times: History of the 144th new york infantry. New York: H.E. Bailey.

Marcot, R. (2007). U.S. Sharpshooters, Berdan's Civil War Elite. Mechanicsburg, PA: Stackpole.

Mattocks, C. (1994). Unspoiled Heart, The Journal of Charles Mattocks of the 17th Maine. Knoxville, TN: University of Tennessee Press .

Medical Society of the State of Pennsylvania. (1910). State News Items. Pennsylvania Medical Journal, 13, p. 386.

Mellish, E. W. (1962). Empire State Society of the National Society Sons of the American Revolution Application for Membership. New York.

Moody, J. (1899). The war of the rebellion: a compilation of the official records of the Union and Confederate armies. ; Series 3 - Volume 1. Washington D.C.: Government Printing Office.

Mott, H. (1921, April). Josiah Collins Pumpelly. New York Genealogical and Biographical Record, pp. 105-108.

Murray, R. (2005). Letters from Berdan's Sharpshooters. Wolcott, NY: Benedum Books.

National Archives and Records Administration. (2008). Carmick, Edward J WC78118. Retrieved from Fold3.com: http://www.fold3.com/image/249/279945697/

National Archives and Records Administration. (2008). Phelps, David WC61331. Retrieved from Fold3.com: http://www.fold3.com/image/249/271166574/

National Park Service. (1999). Andersonville Prisoner of War Database. Provo, UT. Retrieved April 23, 2013, from http://search.ancestrylibrary.com/search/db.aspx?dbid=3708&enc=1

New York, Town Clerks' Registers of Men Who Served in the Civil War, ca 1861-1865. (n.d.). Provo, UT. Retrieved April 24, 2013, from http://search.ancestrylibrary.com/iexec?htx=View&r=5542&dbid=1964&iid=31513_216251-00432&fn=George+M&ln=Barber&st=r&ssrc=&pid=66375

Peet, F. T. (1896). Empire State Society of the Sons of the American Revolution. New York: Board of Managers of the Empire State Society.

Peet, F. T. (1896, March 7). Letter to Hugh Hastings. Albany, New York.

Peet, F. T. (1905). Personal Experiences in the Civil War. New York: F.T. Peet.

Peet, F. T. (1917). Civil War Letters and Documents of Frederick Tomlinson Peet. New York: Newport.

Person, G. (2008). Answering the Call: the New York State Militia Responds to the Crisis of 1861. Civil War Historian, 1-13.

Philadelphia City Archives. (2010). Philadelphia, Pennsylvania, Death Certificates Index, 1803-1915. Provo UT: Ancestry.com.

Phillips, M. (2006, Apr 12). H W Ecker. Retrieved Jan 6, 2014, from findagrave.com: http://www.findagrave.com/cgi-bin/fg.cgi?page=gr&GSln=ecker&GSfn=h&GSmn=w&GSbyrel=all&GSdyrel=all&GSob=n&GRid=13925429&df=all&

Phoenix, S. W. (1878). The Whitney Family of Connecticut. New York: Privately Printed.

Pierce, F. (1896). Fiske and Fisk Family. Chicago, IL: W.B. Conkey Company.

Porter, F. J. (1862, October 23). Special Order no. 157. Sharpsburg, MD: War Department.

Porter, F.-J. (1887). Report of Maj. Gen. Fitz-John Porter, U. S. Army, commanding Fifth Army Corps, of the battle of Antietam, skirmish at Blackford's or Boteler's Ford, and action near Shepherdstown. In R. N. Scott, War of the Rebellion: A compilation of the Official Records of the Union and Confederate Armies (pp. 338-341). Washington D.C.: Government Printing Office.

Powtin, T. S. (1894). Yale Class of 1851 for Forty Years. Boston: A. Mudge and Sons.

Provost Marshal General's Bureau . (n.d.). U.S., Civil War Draft Registrations Records, 1863-1865. Retrieved from Ancestry.com: http://search.ancestrylibrary.com/cgi-bin/sse.dll?rank=1&new=1&MSAV=0&msT=1&gss=angs-g&gsfn=John&gsln=bala&msbdy=1831&msbpn__ftp=newport+herkimer&msrpn__ftp=new+york&uidh=m23&mssng0=catherine&pcat=ROOT_CATEGORY&h=4213244&db=ConsolidatedListsofCivilWarReg&

Purdy, E. (2002). The Final Civil War Diary of Charles B. Mead of Company F First U.S. Sharpshooters. Rutland Historical Society Quarterly, 32.

Ragan, G. (2009, Dec 3). Pvt. Theodore Stanwood Nash. Retrieved Jan 6,

2014, from findagrave.com: http://www.findagrave.com/cgi-bin/fg.cgi?page=gr&GSln=nash&GSfn=t&GSmn=s&GSbyrel=all&GSdy=1898&GSdyrel=in&GSob=n&GRid=45053398&df=all&

Records of the Department of Veterans Affairs. (n.d.). War of 1812 Pension Application Files Index, 1812-1815. Retrieved April 23, 2013, from Ancestry.com: http://search.ancestrylibrary.com/cgi-bin/sse.dll?rank=1&new=1&MSAV=0&msT=1&gss=angs-c&gsfn=orange&gsln=doty&uidh=m23&pcat=39&h=95682&recoff=6+7&db=Warof1812_Pension&indiv=1

Reynolds, C. (1911). Hudson Mohawk Genealogical and Family Memoirs (Vol. II). New York: Lewis Historical Publishing Company.

Rhea, G. (2007). Cold Harbor. Baton Rouge: LSU Press.

Robin. (2006, Jul 13). Noah A Olds. Retrieved Jan 6, 2014, from findagrave: http://www.findagrave.com/cgi-bin/fg.cgi?page=gr&GSln=olds&GSfn=noah&GSbyrel=all&GSdyrel=all&GSob=n&GRid=14923071&df=all&

Roecker, G. (2010, Aug 19). Pvt. Ramsey Black. Retrieved Jan 6, 2014, from findagrave.com: http://www.findagrave.com/cgi-bin/fg.cgi?page=gr&GSln=black&GSfn=r&GSbyrel=all&GSdy=1862&GSdyrel=in&GSob=n&GRid=57343907&df=all&

Rohwedder, B. (2009, July 15). Henry Niles. Retrieved Jan 6, 2014, from findagrave.com: http://www.findagrave.com/cgi-bin/fg.cgi?page=gr&GSln=niles&GSfn=henry&GSbyrel=all&GSdyrel=all&GSob=n&GRid=39473464&df=all&

Saar, E. (2007, Oct 1). George A Livingston. Retrieved Jan 6, 2014, from findagrave: http://www.findagrave.com/cgi-bin/fg.cgi?page=gr&GSln=livingston&GSfn=george&GSmn=a&GSbyrel=all&GSdyrel=all&GSob=n&GRid=21873333&df=all&

Sabin, C. E. (1956). Colorado Society of the National Society of the Sons of the American Revolution.

Schenck, E. (1889). The history of Fairfield, Fairfield County, Connecticut, from the Settlement of the Town in 1639 to 1818. Fairfield, CT: By the Author.

(1898). Testimony of Joseph TH Hall. In U. Senate, Examination of the Civil Service (pp. 175-178). Washington D.C.: Government Printing Office.

Sharfstein, D. (2011). The Invisible Line. New York: Penguin Press.

Shaw, R. G. (1999). Blue Eyed Child of Fortune: The Civil War Letters of Robert Gould Shaw. Athens, GA: University of Georgia Press.

Shipgoer. (2000, Feb 26). James M Thorn. Retrieved Jan 6, 2014, from findagrave.com: http://www.findagrave.com/cgi-bin/fg.cgi?page=gr&GSln=thorn&GSfn=james&GSmn=m&GSbyrel=all&GSdyrel=all&GSob=n&GRid=1253220&df=all&

Shipgoer. (2000, Feb 25). Slyvester Lawson. Retrieved Jan 6, 2014, from findagrave: http://www.findagrave.com/cgi-bin/fg.cgi?page=gr&GSln=lawson&GSfn=sylvester&GSbyrel=all&GSdyrel=all&GSob=n&GRid=907184&df=all&

Skillman, B. (2002). What did they Wear? A post-Gettysburg analysis of Clothing and Equipment requisitioned by the 1st USSS on July 28, 1863.

Skillman, B., Carey, J., & White, B. (2012). Who were they? The 1st Regiment U.S. Sharpshooter Armorers.

Skinner, R. (1830). New York State Register for the year of our lord 1830. New York: Clayton and Van Norden.

Smallwood-Roberts, R. L. (2012, Oct 5). John T. Schermerhorn. Retrieved Jan 6, 2014, from findagrave.com: http://www.findagrave.com/cgi-bin/fg.cgi?page=gr&GSln=schermerhorn&GSfn=john&GSmn=t&GSbyrel=all&GSdyrel=all&GSob=n&GRid=98329011&df=all&

Smithsonian Institute. (2013, April 29). Civil War @ Smithsonian. Retrieved from The Smithsonian Institute: http://www.civilwar.si.edu/soldiering_berdan_uniform.html#

Stedman, T. (1910). Obituary Notes. Medical Record, 77, p. 200.

Steed. (2012, Feb 4). George Brinkerhoff Pumpelly. Retrieved Jan 6, 2014, from findagrave: http://www.findagrave.com/cgi-bin/fg.cgi?page=gr&GSln=pumpelly&GSfn=george&GSbyrel=all&GSdyrel=all&GSob=n&GRid=84462496&df=all&

Stevens, C. A. (1892). Berdan's Sharpshooters in the Army of the Potomac. St. Paul MN.

Stiles, H. (1867). A History of the city of Brooklyn: Including the old town and village of Brooklyn, the town of Bushwick, and the village and city of Williamsburgh. New York.

Stiles, H. R. (1870). A History of the City of Brooklyn Volume 3. New York: Published by Subscription.

Swinton, W. (1870). History of the Seventh Regiment, National Guard, State of New York, during the War of the Rebellion. New York: Fields, Osgood & Co. .

T., L. (2000, Mar 4). Jacob Crawford. Retrieved Jan 6, 2014, from findagrave.com: http://www.findagrave.com/cgi-bin/fg.cgi?page=gr&GSln=crawford&GSfn=jacob&GSbyrel=all&GSdyrel=all&GSob=n&GRid=3060869&df=all&

Templarion. (2009, Aug 6). Robert William Helms. Retrieved Jan 6, 2014, from findagrave.com: http://www.findagrave.com/cgi-bin/fg.cgi?page=gr&GSln=helms&GSfn=robert&GSmn=w&GSbyrel=all&GSdyrel=all&GSob=n&GRid=40369287&df=all&

Terwilliger, J. (1868). Calendar of Historical Manuscripts Relating to the War of the Revolution. Albany, NY: Weed, Parsons and Co. .

Tousley, J. R. (1968). Board of Managers of the Sons of the American Revolution. Independence, OH.

Trepp, C. (1862). Report of Lieutant Colonel Casper Trepp, First US Sharpshooter. Washington D.C.: Government Printing Office.

Trepp, C. (1863, August 12). Letter Received by the Commission Branch of the Adjutant General's Office. Sulpher Springs, VA.

Trepp, C. (1863). Report of Lieutenant Colonel Casper Trepp, First US Sharpshooters #150. Washington, D.C.: Goverment Printing Office.

Ubaudi, B. (2001, Sept 27). Descendants of Charles Queen. Retrieved from http://familytreemaker.genealogy.com/users/u/b/a/Bob-Ubaudi/GENE56-0019.html

United States Census Bureau. (1890). Surviving Soldiers , Sailors, and Marines, and Widows etc. Washington D.C. Retrieved May 7, 2013, from http://search.ancestrylibrary.com/iexec?htx=View&r=5542&dbid=8667&iid=VAM123_106-0447&fn=George&ln=Simmons&st=r&ssrc=&pid=35425

University of Oregon. (n.d.). Life Expectancy Graphs. Retrieved May 7, 2013, from Mapping History: http://mappinghistory.uoregon.edu/english/US/US39-01.html

US Census Bureau. (1850). Alexandria, Jefferson, New York; Roll: M432_515. Washington, D.C.: Government Printing Office.

US Census Bureau. (1850). Austerlitz, Columbia, New York; Roll: M432_492. Washington, D.C.: Government Printing Office.

US Census Bureau. (1850). Brooklyn Ward 1, Kings, New York, Roll: M432-517. Washington, D.C.: Government Printing Office.

US Census Bureau. (1850). Germantown, Columbia, New York; Roll: M432_492. Washington, D.C.: Government Printing Office.

US Census Bureau. (1850). Huntington, Suffolk, New York; Roll: M432_601. Washington, D.C.: Government Printing Office.

US Census Bureau. (1850). Huntington, Suffolk, New York; Roll: M432_601. Washington, D.C.: Government Printing Office.

US Census Bureau. (1850). Islip, Suffolk, New York; Roll: M432_601. Washington, D.C.: US Government Printing Office.

US Census Bureau. (1850). Islip, Suffolk, New York; Roll: M432_601. Washington, D.C.: Government Printing Office.

US Census Bureau. (1850). Johnstown, Fulton, New York; Roll: M432_506. Washington, D.C.: Government Printing Office.

US Census Bureau. (1850). Keene, Essex, New York RollM432-503. Washington D.C.: Government Printing Office.

US Census Bureau. (1850). Kingsbury, Washington, New York Roll M432-610. Washington, DC: US Government Printing Office.

US Census Bureau. (1850). New Haven, New Haven, Connecticut; Roll: M432_47. Washington, D.C.: Government Printing Office.

US Census Bureau. (1850). New York Ward 11, New York, New York; Roll: M432_547. Washington, D.C.: Government Printing Office.

US Census Bureau. (1850). New York Ward 14, New York, New York; Roll: M432_551. Washington, D.C.: Government Printing Office.

US Census Bureau. (1850). North Bergen, Hudson, New Jersey; Roll: M432_452. Washington, D.C.: Government Printing Office.

US Census Bureau. (1850). Norway, Herkimer, New York; Roll: M432_513. Washington, D.C.: Government Printing Office.

US Census Bureau. (1850). Owego, Tioga, New York; Roll: M432_604. Washington, D.C.: Government Printing Office.

US Census Bureau. (1850). Oyster Bay, Queens, New York; Roll: M432_582. Washington, D.C.: Government Printing Office.

US Census Bureau. (1850). Smithfield, Madison, New York; Roll: M432_526. Washington, D.C.: Government Printing Office.

US Census Bureau. (1850). Willsboro, Essex, New York; Roll: M432_503. Washington, D.C.: Government Printing Office.

US Census Bureau. (1860). Brooklyn Ward 3 District 1, Kings, New York; Roll: M653_764. Washington, D.C.: Government Printing Office.

US Census Bureau. (1860). Castleton, Richmond, New York Roll: m653_850. Washington, D.C.: Government Printing Office.

US Census Bureau. (1860). Chatham, Columbia, New York; Roll: M653_738. Washington, D.C.: Government Printing Office.

US Census Bureau. (1860). Clarkstown, Rockland, New York; Roll: M653_851. Washington D.C.: Government Printing Office.

US Census Bureau. (1860). Huntington, Suffolk, New York; Roll: M653_864. Washington, D.C.: Government Printing Office.

US Census Bureau. (1860). Huntington, Suffolk, New York; Roll: M653_864. Washington, D.C.: Government Printing Office.

US Census Bureau. (1860). Huntington, Suffolk, New York; Roll: M653_864. Washington, D.C.: Government Printing Office.

US Census Bureau. (1860). Jay, Essex, New York; Roll: M653_753. Washington, D.C.: Government Printing Office.

US Census Bureau. (1860). Jay, Essex, New York; Roll: M653_753. Washington, D.C.: Government Printing Office.

US Census Bureau. (1860). Johnstown, Fulton, New York; Roll: M653_755. Washington, D.C.: Government Printing Office.

US Census Bureau. (1860). Milo, Yates, New York; Roll: M653_885. Washington, D.C.: Government Printing Office.

US Census Bureau. (1860). New York Ward 11 District 3, New York, New York; Roll: M653_799. Washington, D.C.: Government Printing Office.

US Census Bureau. (1860). New York Ward 22 District 2, New York, New York; Roll: M653_820. Washington, D.C.: Government Printing Office.

US Census Bureau. (1860). New York Ward 5, New York, New York; Roll: M432_537. Washington, D.C.: Government Printing Office.

US Census Bureau. (1860). Newburgh, Orange, New York; Roll: M653_834. Washington, D.C.: Government Printing Office.

US Census Bureau. (1860). Newport, Herkimer, New York; Roll: M653_759. Washington, D.C.: Government Printing Office.

US Census Bureau. (1860). Newport, Herkimer, New York; Roll: M653_759. Washington, D.C.: Government Printing Office.

US Census Bureau. (1860). Norway, Herkimer, New York; Roll: M653_760. Washington, D.C.: Government Printing Office.

US Census Bureau. (1860). Owego, Tioga, New York; Roll: M653_867. Washington, D.C.: Government Printing Office.

US Census Bureau. (1860). Pawling, Dutchess, New York; Roll: M653_741. Washington, D.C.: Government Printing Office.

US Census Bureau. (1860). Potter, Yates, New York; Roll: M653_885. Washington, D.C.: Government Printing Office.

US Census Bureau. (1860). Raritan, Monmouth, New Jersey; Roll: M653_701. Washington, D.C.: Government Printing Office.

US Census Bureau. (1860). Schenectady Ward 1, Schenectady, New York; Roll: M653_858. Washington, D.C.: Government Printing Office.

US Census Bureau. (1860). Seneca Falls, Seneca, New York; Roll: M653_861. Washington, D.C.: Government Printing Office.

US Census Bureau. (1860). Theresa, Jefferson, New York; Roll: M653_762. Washington, D.C.: Government Printing Office.

US Census Bureau. (1860). Willsboro, Essex, New York; Roll: M653_753. Washington, D.C.: Government Printing Office.

US Census Bureau. (1860). Willsboro, Essex, New York; Roll: M653_753. Washington, D.C.: Government Printing Office.

US Census Bureau. (1870). Austerlitz, Columbia, New York; Roll: M593_920. Washington, D.C.: Government Printing Office.

US Census Bureau. (1870). Brooklyn Ward 21, Kings, New York; Roll: M593_961. Washington, D.C.: Government Printing Office.

US Census Bureau. (1870). Crystal, Tama, Iowa; Roll: M593_420. Washington D.C.: Government Printing Office.

US Census Bureau. (1870). Jersey City Ward 12, Hudson, New Jersey; Roll: M593_868. Washington, D.C.: Government Printing Office.

US Census Bureau. (1870). Kirkwood, Broome, New York; Roll: M593_907. Washington, D.C.: Government Printing Office.

US Census Bureau. (1870). New York City, New York, New York; Roll: 896. Washington, D.C.: Government Printing Office.

US Census Bureau. (1870). New York Ward 8 District 15, New York, New York; Roll: M593_981. Washington, D.C.: Government Printing Office.

US Census Bureau. (1870). Oyster Bay, Queens, New York; Roll: M593_1081. Washington, D.C.: Government Printing Office.

US Census Bureau. (1870). Pawling, Dutchess, New York; Roll: M593_926. Washington, D.C.: Government Printing Office.

US Census Bureau. (1870). Saratoga, Saratoga, New York; Roll: M593_1088. Washington, D.C.: Government Printing Office.

US Census Bureau. (1870). Washington Ward 1, Washington, District of Columbia; Roll: M593_123. Washington, D.C.: Government Printing Office.

US Census Bureau. (1870). West Troy, Albany, New York; Roll: M593_903. Washington, D.C.: Government Printing Office.

US Census Bureau. (1880). Brasher Falls, St Lawrence, New York; Roll: 925. Washington, D.C.: Government Printing Office.

US Census Bureau. (1880). Brooklyn, Kings, New York; Roll: 853. Washington, D.C.: Government Printing Office.

US Census Bureau. (1880). Brooklyn, Kings, New York; Roll: 857. Washington, D.C.: Government Printing Office.

US Census Bureau. (1880). Fairbury, Jefferson, Nebraska; Roll: 750. Washington, D.C.: Government Printing Office.

US Census Bureau. (1880). Indianapolis, Marion, Indiana Roll: 296. Washington, D.C.: Government Printing Office.

US Census Bureau. (1880). Lyons, Wayne, New York; Roll: 944. Washington, D.C.: Government Printing Office.

US Census Bureau. (1880). Mount Vernon, Fairfax, Virginia; Roll: 1364. Washington, D.C.: Government Printing Office.

US Census Bureau. (1880). North Bergen, Hudson, New Jersey; Roll: 785. Washington, D.C.: Government Printing Office.

US Census Bureau. (1880). Norway, Herkimer, New York; Roll: 838. Washington, D.C.: Government Printing Office.

US Census Bureau. (1880). Paterson, Passaic, New Jersey; Roll: 796. Washington, D.C.: Government Printing Office.

US Census Bureau. (1880). Philadelphia, Philadelphia, Pennsylvania; Roll: 1173. Washington, D.C.: Government Printing Office.

US Census Bureau. (1880). Queens, Queens, New York; Roll: 919. Washington, D.C.: US Government Printing Office.

US Census Bureau. (1880). Westport, Essex, New York; Roll: 833. Washington, D.C.: Government Printing Office.

US Census Bureau. (1900). Babylon, Suffolk, New York; Roll: 1165. Washington, D.C.: Government Printing Office.

US Census Bureau. (1900). Chatham, Columbia, New York; Roll: 1019. Washington, D.C.: Government Printing Office.

US Census Bureau. (1900). Islip, Suffolk, New York; Roll: 1165. Washington, D.C.: Government Printing Office.

US Census Bureau. (1900). Jay, Essex, New York; Roll: 1035. Washington, D.C.: Government Printing Office.

US Census Bureau. (1900). Norwalk, Fairfield, Connecticut; Roll: 134;. Washington, D.C.: Government Printing Office.

US Census Bureau. (1900). Rubicon, Huron, Michigan; Roll: 715. Washington, D.C.: Government Printing Office.

US Census Bureau. (1910). Brooklyn Ward 28, Kings, New York; Roll: T624_982. Washington, D.C.: Government Printing Office.

US Census Bureau. (1910). Newark Ward 2, Essex, New Jersey; Roll: T624_876. Washington, D.C.: Government Printing Office.

US Census Bureau. (1910). Pleasant Valley, Fayette, Iowa; Roll: T624_402. Washington, D.C.: Government Printing Office.

US Census Bureau. (1910). Wilmington, Will, Illinois; Roll: T624_335. Washington, D.C.: Government Printing Office.

US Census Bureau. (1920). Census Place: Newark Ward 16, Essex, New Jersey; Roll: T625_1038. Washington, D.C.: Government Printing Office.

Weston, R. (1863). Special Order. Virginia.

Weygant, C. H. (1877). History of the 124th Regiment NYSV. Newburgh, NY: Journal Printing House.

Whitney, H. C. (1922, September 8). U.S., Sons of the American Revolution Membership Applications, 1889-1970 Record for Darling Whitney. Retrieved May 8, 2013, from Ancestry.com: http://search.ancestrylibrary.com/iexec?htx=View&r=5542&dbid=2204&iid=32596_242204-00404&fn=Darling&ln=Whitney&st=r&ssrc=&pid=454924

wienerin. (2001, June 8). John J Bala. Retrieved Jan 6, 2014, from findagrave.com: http://www.findagrave.com/cgi-bin/fg.cgi?page=gr&GSln=bala&GSfn=john&GSbyrel=all&GSdyrel=all&GSob=n&GRid=71025481&df=all&

Wilcox, D. (2011, Dec 12). Dr. George F. Hall. Retrieved Jan 6, 2014, from findagrave: http://www.findagrave.com/cgi-bin/fg.cgi?page=gr&GSln=hall&GSfn=george&GSmn=f&GSbyrel=all&GSdy=1896&GSdyrel=in&GSob=n&GRid=81670494&df=all&

Wiley, B. I. (2008). Life of Billy Yank. Baton Rouge, LA: Louisiana State University Press.

Williams, D. (2005, Sep 2). Pvt. David Phelps. Retrieved Jan 6, 2014, from findagrave: http://www.findagrave.com/cgi-bin/fg.cgi?page=gr&GSln=phelps&GSfn=david&GSbyrel=all&GSdy=1862&GSdyrel=in&GSob=n&GRid=11663237&df=all&

Winthrop, W. (1863, February 18). Camp Near Falmouth . Falmouth, VA: National Archives and Records Administration.

Winthrop, W. (1863, February 6). Camp near Falmouth VA. Falmouth, VA: National Archives and Records Administration.

Wohler, M. (2011, Jul 4). Philip Service. Retrieved Jan 6, 2014, from findagrave: http://www.findagrave.com/cgi-bin/fg.cgi?page=gr&GSln=service&GSfn=philip&GSbyrel=all&GSdyrel=all&GSob=n&GRid=72701238&df=all&

Wolfe, J. (2013, February 16). Family Notes for Thomas Hicks and Mary Doughty. Retrieved May 14, 2013, from Thomas Hicks: http://www-personal.umich.edu/~bobwolfe/gen/mn/m5434x5406.htm

wtoomey. (2006, Aug 24). Corp N Rouse. Retrieved Jan 6, 2014, from findagrave.com: http://www.findagrave.com/cgi-bin/fg.cgi?page=gr&GSln=rouse&GSfn=n&GSbyrel=all&GSdyrel=all&GSob=n&GRid=15486619&df=all&

Young, E. (1899). Proceedings of the massachusetts historical society. (Vol. 6). Boston: Massachusetts Historical Society.

Company H exists today through the hard work and dedication of reenactors:

Visit the website for more pictures, grave markers and information about Company H.

https://www.facebook.com/nyberdans

Company H, reenacted at the 1st US Sharpshooters (New York Companies) Monument, Gettysburg PA